The Evolution of Spanish

Juan de la Cuesta
Hispanic Monographs

Insert for *The Evolution of Spanish*

☞ To Avoid Confusion ☜

THERE ARE SOME lingering typographical errors in the book, some of which might easily confuse·the novice historical grammarian if unfixed; they are the ones that have been listed below. A few other obvious ones, for example *thw* for *the,* have not been mentioned.

PAGE AND LINE	READS	SHOULD READ
6, 17 up	[U] as in Sp. 'uso'	[U] as in English 'look'
		[u] as in Spanish 'uso'
16, 7 up	'I fall': 'I fall down'	'I fall'; óccidō 'I fall down'
27, 17	facia, 3rd.	facie, 3rd
33, 1 up	neuter [-ae, -o]	neuter [-o]
63, 6	complicated the	complicated than the
68, 12 up	foz	foze
69, 6	the -e	the -e remained.
75, 10 up	*and* the preceding vowel.	*and* the preceding consonant.
78, 10 up	ceresa	cereza
78, 8-9 up	delete	
82, 4 ff.	λ	·λy
86, 4	[δ, γ]	[β, δ]
97, 16	[č]	[x]
98, 13	stercolre	stercore
107, 6 up	foedam	foedum
113, 12 up	*veínte*	*véinte*
116, 1 up	[muʒ'ar]	[muʒɛr]
119, 1 up	con-	consis-
124, 12 up	third person singular is	third person plural
126, 8	dīcŏre	dīcĕre
129, 19 up	(The *u*	(The *y*
130, 9 up	VL and	VL ant
131, 20	clames > llame	clames > llames
134, 11 up	CL stēmus > Sp. estemos	CL stētis > Sp. estéis
138, 6	vistieno	vistiendo
140, 15	eřrāmus	ĕrāmus
140, 17	̆rant	ĕrant

The Evolution of Spanish

An Introductory Historical Grammar

BY

Thomas A. Lathrop

University of Delaware

Juan de la Cuesta
Newark, Delaware

To my parents

DONALD C. LATHROP
and
ETHEL M. LATHROP

For their Encouragement and Enthusiasm

Contents

❧ Introduction ❦

WHEN I BEGAN TO STUDY the evolution of the Spanish language a number of years ago, I would have liked to find a concise historical grammar written in English and designed for the novice. I searched with diligence but without success for such a volume. Later, as a professor of the same subject, I sought the same sort of book for my students' use, but still none could be found. It was then that I resolved to write this volume myself.

Since the university student who becomes interested in the Spanish language frequently does not come equipped with a knowledge of Classical Latin, the book's first chapter deals with the major features of this language, especially with those which are important to the development of Spanish. At the same time, it also describes the workings of Vulgar Latin—the spoken language of the masses. It was, after all, this spoken, simplified version of Latin, and not Classical Latin, which gave rise to the Romance Languages.

The second chapter treats historical phonetics—the evolution of sounds—from Latin to Spanish. It assumes that the reader does not know the definitions or mechanics of the various processes that cause phonetic change, so each new feature or technical term is defined as it arises. In addition, a great many examples illustrate each point, and these examples are clearly set off.

The third and final chapter deals with historical morphology—the development of nouns, adjectives, verbs, and so on—from Latin to Spanish, again with what I hope are good explanations and sufficient examples.

The difficult part about putting this manuscript together was in deciding what to commit to print, and what to pass over in silence; what to explain in detail, what to simplify, and what to mention merely in passing. It is obvious that since language is the most complex invention of man, the development of a language must of necessity be an extraordinarily complicated subject, worthy of a series of volumes; this abbreviated manual cannot, therefore, begin to answer every question. Its purpose is only to introduce the novice historical grammarian to some of the facts and problems of the development of Spanish and to prepare him or her for a more detailed study in the masterworks of Spanish historical grammar.

Since the object of the book is to describe the development of standard Spanish, it would be inappropriate to complicate and confuse issues by discussing dialectal developments. Dialectal features have been mentioned on just a few occasions, and then only in passing. On the other hand, it seems both appropriate and useful to discuss Old Spanish developments when they contrast with or shed light on modern forms.

Likewise, since the goal of historcial grammar is to trace the evolution of a language, this book focuses attention virtually exclusively on 'traditional' developments, and excludes almost entirely 'learned borrowings', since the latter by definition, do not contribute to the understanding of the evolution of the language. A 'traditional' word is one that has been in constant use (and therefore in constant evolution) from the days when Latin was spoken until the present. On the other hand, a 'learned borrowing' is a word which has been plucked in relatively recent times from Classical Latin vocabulary and integrated into the modern idiom merely with a change or two in spelling to conform to the current norm. Frequently, both a 'traditional' development and a 'learned borrowing' deriving from the *same* Latin word exist side by side in modern Spanish. For example, the traditional development of Latin *artĭcŭlum* is *artejo* 'knuckle' (through a regular series of phonetic changes). The same Latin word has also given the learned *artículo* merely through the substitution of *-o* for the Latin *-um*. The reader should not be distressed, then, to find *artejo* listed as the only development of *artĭcŭlum* (§§9, 77, 98, 102, 142), while no mention is made of the learned *artículo*.

Finally, it must be said that although Latin forms the foundation of Spanish, other languages, notably Arabic, Basque, and the Germanic group, have contributed considerably to Spanish vocabulary. Since the scope of this book includes only the Latin element, it is hoped that the reader will consult other books for information about the non-Latin influences on Spanish. Some excellent sources in English are Professor W. J. Entwistle's *The Spanish Language* and Professor R. K. Spaulding's *How Spanish Grew*; in Spanish, Professor Rafael Lapesa's monumental *Historia de la lengua española* is the standard text.

⚘   ⚘

I would like to thank various people for their encouragement or helpful comments at various stages of the production of the work. Those people who read the typescript in its entirety include: Professor Gerhard Probst of the University of Berlin, who was especially helpful in matters of Classical Latin culture; Professor Richard Abraham of the University of Miami, whose kind words were greatly appreciated; Professor Richard Kinkade of the University of Connecticut, who read the work in an earlier version, and whose critique helped to shape this final format; and Martha Shopmyer, who, while she was my student, offered comments from the undergraduate's point of view. While the Latin chapter was being written, Professor Marie Helmer, a Classicist and researcher who works in Madrid, answered numerous queries about Classical Latin morphology. When the chapter was finished it was read by Professor Richard O. Hale of the University of North Dakota, and by Professor Howard Marblestone, a polyglot-scholar of Allentown, Pennsylvania. Professor Fredrick Agard of Cornell University offered a valuable critique about a variant of the present chapter about Latin. The final two chapters were read by Professor Frede Jensen of the University of Colorado, my mentor in Romance Philology. I must confess that I did not take every one of the suggestions made by my friends and colleagues listed above, and I alone am responsible for any lingering infelicities in the text.

I should also like to express my gratitude to the scholars, whose works and words I have freely drawn upon. The books listed in the BIBLIOGRAPHY by Professors Väänänen, da Silva Neto, Maurer and Elcock are responsible for much of the information about Classical and Vulgar Latin. And for the second and third chapters, I have most freely and most often drawn on the works by Ramón Menéndez Pidal; indeed, I often wonder if the Spanish language would have a history at all if it weren't for this scholar. I should also like to thank Professor Samuel G. Armistead of the University of Pennsylvania, whose lucid classes in historical grammar gave me a foundation in this field.

I am greatly indebted to the Del Amo Foundation of Los Angeles, California, whose generous research grant allowed me to prepare this book in Madrid. While there, I was priviledged to use the fine library and other facilities of the Casa de Velazquez, and this greatly facilitated the entire project. I would like to thank the Director of the Casa de Velazquez, François Chevalier, for his kindness. Finally, I thank my wife, Connie, who read the entire project as it was being written, and whose expertise in matters of Romance historical grammar kept a great number of *bêtises* from leaving the family.

T. A. L.

Newark, Delaware
August, 1980

Vowels

[i] as in Spanish sí
[ɪ] as in English bit
[e] as in Spanish quepo
[ɛ] as in Spanish sentar
[a] as in Spanish hablo
[ɔ] as is Spanish flor
[o] as is Spanish cómo
[ʊ] as is English look
[u] as is Spanish lugar
[y] as in Spanish siento
[w] as in Spanish bueno

A subscript hook under a vowel means that is it open.
A subscript dot under a vowel means that it is close.

ị = [i]		ọ = [ɔ]
į = [ɪ]		o̦ = [o]
ẹ = [e]		u̦ = [ʊ]
ę = [ɛ]		ụ = [u]

Consonants

[p] as in Spanish pierna	[θ] as in Spanish cinco (Spain)
[t] as in Spanish tomar	[s] as in Spanish sed
[k] as in Spanish casa	[z] as in English zebra
[b] as in Spanish hambre	[š] as in English ship
[d] as in Spanish andar	[ʒ] as in English leisure
[g] as in Spanish tengo	[č] as in Spanish chico
[β] as in Spanish haber	[ǯ] as in English jump
[δ] as in Spanish bledo	[x] as in Spanish ajo
[γ] as in Spanish hago	[λy] as in Spanish calle (Spain)
[f] as in Spanish favor	

❧ 1 ❧

The Heritage of Vulgar Latin

§1. While the educated Romans were speaking and writing according to the rules of the Classical Latin language (*sermo urbanus*), the largely uneducated populace—the soldiers of lower rank, merchants, and laborers—were speaking (and writing, if they possessed that skill) a less complex, pedestrian version of the language which we know as Vulgar Latin (*sermo vulgaris*).[1]

When Rome fell towards the end of the fourth century A.D., the educated ruling class disappeared, and with it the educated spoken and written language, Classical Latin, also faded away. But Vulgar Latin, spoken by the masses in the huge area between Lusitania and Dacia (modern Portugal and Romania), was easily able to survive the fall of the distant capital, and the disappearance of the Classical tongue—spoken by a very small portion of the Empire's population—went largely unnoticed by the masses. It was therefore Vulgar Latin and *not* Classical Latin, which was to evolve day by day, century by century, into the modern Romance Languages.

Vulgar Latin differed from Classical Latin on all linguistic levels. Its vowels were quite distinct from Classical vowels, and its consonants showed certain deviations as well. Vulgar Latin nouns and verbs were more simply organized than, or differed from, their Classical equivalents, and because of these differences, a number of changes had to take place in Vulgar Latin syntax. In its vocabulary, Vulgar Latin preferred the emphatic, expressive and diminutive words of its Classical counterpart, and, as a result,

---

[1] Vulgar Latin is traditionally divided into Western and Eastern halves. Eastern Vulgar Latin gave rise to the 'Eastern' Romance Languages (Italian and Romanian), and Western Vulgar Latin gave rise to the 'Western' Romance Languages (French, Spanish, Portuguese and Catalan).

many of the less forceful and less picturesque Classical words were not retained. Finally, Vulgar Latin readily assimilated foreign words of diverse origin into its vocabulary, unlike Classical Latin which accepted only a few, mostly from Greek.

If Vulgar Latin was the *spoken* language of largely *illiterate* speakers who spent their lives in the low military ranks, in the marketplaces, or at construction sites, how can we have any notion of what their *spoken* language was like?

Surprisingly, there is quite a bit of information about Vulgar Latin which survives in a number of written sources, but mostly in bits and pieces.

One would think that the least likely place to look for data concerning Vulgar Latin would be in the works of Classical authors, yet there are a few good sources. In the comedies of Plautus (ca. 254-184 B.C.) some of the characters are modeled after 'the man in the street', and when they speak, we observe glimpses of Vulgar Latin. The first century satirist, Petronius, in his famous *Cena Trimalchionis* 'Trimalchio's Feast', describes a colorful banquet attended by the lower classes of society, and in the characters' bawdy language we can see traits of Vulgar Latin.

Turning to the works of untrained writers who arose from the populace, one would naturally expect to see the authors' speech habits reflected in their work, and such was indeed the case. A good example of this is the *Peregrinatio ad loca sancta* 'Pilgrimage to Holy Places', a description of the travels of a nun to the Holy Land in the early centuries of our era. The author's Latin prose anticipates some of the structures that the Romance Languages would adopt and discards some that would be later rejected by the Romance Languages.

There were a few treatises written by specialists who were qualified in their fields, but not so well qualified in the Classical idiom, and from these we can also find information about Vulgar speech. *Mulomedicina Chironis* was a manual written by the fourth century veterinarian Chiro, in which he explains how to recognize and cure a number of afflictions that might befall a mule. A chef of the same period named Apicius wrote a cookbook, *De re coquinaria*, which has both linguistic and culinary interest. (Professor Veikko Väänänen, a famous authority on Vulgar Latin, reports that these recipies really work.) During the earlier Augustan period (43 B.C. to 13 A.D.) there lived a master architect named Vitruvius who wrote a treatise called *De Architectura*, ten short books on virtually every aspect of Roman architecture and city planning. Although he said that the architect had to be knowledgeable in many different fields, grammar was not necessarily one of them: "Non architectus potest esse grammaticus." 'It is not an architect who can be a grammarian.'

An extraordinarily rich source of Vulgar Latin is found among various types of inscriptions. In 79 A.D. Vesuvius erupted and a great flow of lava extinguished and sealed up the towns of Pompeii and Herculaneum. But through this terrible natural disaster a great linguistic service was rendered to posterity, because over 5000 precious and ordinarily quite perishable *graffiti* were preserved and have been uncovered virtually on every wall at Pompeii. Proclamations, humorous sayings, curses, shopping lists, campaign notices and the expected coarse phrases were scrawled everywhere. These 'inscriptions' were largely scribbled by the populace, and they provide a rich harvest of facts about Vulgar Latin.

Another type of inscription is epitaphs found on gravestones (which were frequently carved by a barely literate relative of the deceased).

Finally, the *defixionum tabellae* 'execration tablets' contained a rather special type of Vulgar Latin inscription. Curses designed to bring misfortune to one's enemy or rival were carved onto lead tablets, and then these *defixionum tabellae* were placed in graves or thrown into wells where they could there attract the attention of the dark forces.

Medieval wordlists, called glossaries, are yet another valuable (although tardive) source of information about Vulgar Latin. The Glossary of Reichenau (named after the monastery where the document used to be kept) is perhaps the mostly important one for the Romance Languages. The purpose of this list was to explain some 3000 words of the Latin Vulgate Bible[2] which were no longer understood by eighth century readers. The archaic words of the Latin biblical text were glossed (that is, they were *translated*) in the margins with 'contemporary' (eighth century) Vulgar Latin equivalents.

The most precious Vulgar Latin document, however, is the famous *Appendix Probi*, a list of 227 'correct' Classical Latin forms

---

[2] The Vulgate is the Latin Bible prepared in about the year 400 A.D. by St. Jerome. It had been used throughout the Catholic world for a thousand years when it became the official Bible of the Catholic church at the Council of Trent in 1546. It is still available, and is now undergoing a thorough revision.

followed by the 'incorrect' Vulgar Latin forms (*say this . . . not this . . .*). It was prepared by a Roman schoolteacher whose mission was to improve the pronunciation and declension skills of his students. However, for modern scholars, this anonymous schoolteacher has left a great wealth of facts about the *lingua franca* of the day. The list of words eventually came to be bound with a manuscript written by the first century grammarian, Probus; thus the list came to be known as the *Appendix Probi* 'Probus' Appendix'.

Examples from the above sources will be seen throughout this chapter to illustrate the various features of Vulgar Latin.

It should be emphasized, however, that many times a Vulgar Latin word that philologists would have *liked* to have found simply does not exist in any known source. In cases such as these, scholars have been able, through a critical comparison of forms taken from the old and modern Romance dialects, to reconstruct what a missing Vulgar Latin form *must have been*. When these reconstructed forms are cited, they are usually preceded by an asterisk to show that the form is hypothetical, or not as yet attested. Many forms which had formerly been 'starred' (i.e., reconstructed), have actually been been attested in later manuscript discoveries, exactly as postulated.[3]

The Vulgar Latin Vocalic System

§2. In Classical Latin there were ten vowels; five were long (nowadays marked with ‾ called 'macron') and five were short (marked with ˘ called 'breve').[4] The difference in the length of vowels was crucial to the meaning of words, as these examples clearly show: *lēgit* (with long *e*) meant 'he read' while *lĕgit* (with short *e*) meant 'he reads'. The noun *ōs* (with long *o*) meant 'mouth' while

---

[3]In this elementary introduction to the development of the language, we felt that making a differentiation between the hypothetical and the attested forms was of little pedagogical use to the novice historical grammarian, and for this reason no asterisks precede any forms in this book. As the reader's philological skills and inquisitiveness grow, he will consult more detailed volumes which will distinguish the unattested forms.

[4] Classical Latin authors used no macrons nor breves. These diacritical marks are a convenience for the modern reader. Usually only the macron is used nowadays, and this book follows the norm; but when the breve is useful for pedagogical purposes, it, too, has been included. In a number of sections, mostly dealing with problems of stress, accent marks have also been included.

ŏs (with short *o*) meant 'bone'. Vowel length affected unstressed as well as stressed vowels, as this example shows: *frūctūs* (with long unstressed final vowel) meant 'fruits' while *frūctŭs* meant 'a fruit'.

§3. In Vulgar Latin, however, vowels were not distinguished by length but by TIMBRE, so that a Classical *long* vowel became a Vulgar Latin CLOSE vowel and a Classical *short* vowel became a Vulgar Latin OPEN vowel.

The notion of close and open vowels can be easily grasped: when a person articulates a close *e* [e] (as in Sp. *quepo*) his mouth is physically more closed than when he articulates an open *e* [ɛ] (as in Sp. *quién*). Similarly, when a person articulates a close *o* [o] (as in Sp. *cosa*), his mouth is more closed than when he articulates the open *o* [ɔ] (as in Sp. *favor*).

The 'vowel triangle',[5] given below, graphically illustrates the arrangement of open and close vowels:

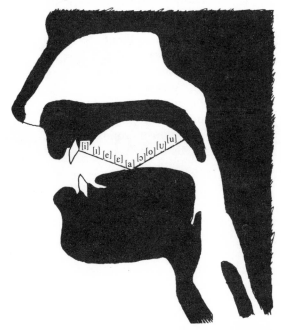

---

[5] The 'vowel triangle' is very useful for pedagogical purposes, but points of articulation do not correspond exactly to the outline given above, as all phoneticians recognize. For more details about points of articulation, the reader can consult Harry Deferrari's *The Phonology of Italian, Spanish and French* (Washington: 1954), and standard phonetics manuals.

While one is pronouncing the sound [i], he cannot put his finger into his mouth since the [i] is articulated too close to his top teeth. When one says [a], his tongue is at its lowest level, affording doctors a nice view of his tonsils. When one produces the [u] sound, the front part of his mouth will be vacant, while his tongue is arched at the back of his mouth. These three points of reference give an idea of the workings of the vowel triangle.

[i], [ɪ], [e], and [ɛ] are called *front vowels* since they are articulated in the front of the mouth; [a] is called a *central vowel*; and, finally, [ɔ], [o], [ʊ], and [u] are called *back vowels*. Similarly, [i] and [u] are called *high vowels* while [e], [ɛ], [o], and [ɔ] are called *mid-vowels*.

If an *e* changes to an *i*, or if an *o* changes to a *u*, they are said to be RAISED since their points of articulation move higher on the vowel triangle. In §§7ab and 17b there are examples of raised vowels.

Here are examples of how these nine vowels sound. The reader is urged to notice his tongue position as he produces these vowels:

[i] as in Spanish 'comí'
[ɪ] as in English 'bit'
[e] as in Spanish 'quepo'
[ɛ] as in Spanish 'quien'
[a] as in Spanish 'hago'
[ɔ] as in Spanish 'color'
[o] as in Spanish 'como'
[ʊ] as in Spanish 'uso'

§4. What follows, then is the development of the vocalic system from Classical Latin to Vulgar Latin.[6] The nine vowels of the vowel triangle represent the initial Western Vulgar Latin result from the ten Classical vowels, but this stage was shortlived since two sets of neighboring vowels were soon to simplify.[7] The open *i* [ɪ] merged with the close *e* [e], and the open *u* merged with the close *o* [ɔ]. The chart below shows this double change:

---

[6] There is a possible polemic here: if Vulgar and Classical Latin were spoken during the same historical period, did Vulgar Latin really develop from Classical Latin at all? or were they two variants of the *same* language (showing the types of differences we see nowadays between the speech of educated versus illiterate people)?

[7] It is important to show both levels of Vulgar Latin vowels here because most inscriptions were written using the vowels given in the first stage of development, yet when the language was spoken, speakers undoubtedly pronounced according to the *second* stage. Readers should bear

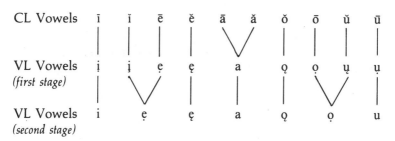

CL līem > VL lite (Sp. lid)
CL vĭces > VL veces (Sp.*veces*)
CL sētam > VL seta (Sp. *seda*)
CL pĕdem > VL pede (Sp. *pie*)
CL prātum > VL pratu (Sp. pr*a*do)
CL nŏvem > VL nove (Sp. n*ue*ve)
CL flōrem > VL flore (Sp. fl*o*r)
CL bŭccam > VL bocca (Sp. b*o*ca)
CL mūrum > VL muru (Sp. m*u*ro)

§5. The three Classical Latin diphthongs (*ae, oe, au*) showed some divergence in Vulgar Latin. The first two (*ae* and *oe*) always simplified (ae > ẹ and oe > ẹ):

CL c*ae*cum > VL cẹcu (Sp. c*ie*go)
CL c*ae*lum > VL cẹlu (Sp. c*ie*lo)
CL f*oe*dam > VL fẹdu (Sp. f*e*o)

However, the diphthong *au* sometimes simplified to open *o* in Vulgar Latin, and sometimes it did not:

CL c*au*sam > VL c*au*sa (Sp. c*o*sa)
CL *au*riculas > VL *o*riclas (Sp. *o*rejas)

This last example is from the *Appendix Probi*: *auriculas non oriclas*.
   a. A few more comments need to be made about the *au*. In Vulgar Latin, if an unstressed *au* was followed by a syllable containing a *u*, the *au* regularly lost its [w] element and simplified to [a]:

---

this disconcerting inconsistency in mind when looking at the Vulgar Latin examples in this book, most of which derive from inscriptions. Perhaps the best way to handle Vulgar Latin would be with a reconstructed pronunciation spelled phonetically, but standard manuals have not used this approach, and we feel it is best to be compatible with them.

CL *auscu*ltare > VL *a*scultare (Sp. escuchar)
CL *augu*stum > VL *a*gustu (Sp. agosto)
CL *augu*rium > VL *a*guriu (Sp. agüero)

The Spanish *escuchar* shows a 'change in prefix' (§157) which accounts for its initial *e*.

b. Finally, an *au* was created in Vulgar Latin by the loss of *-i-* in the third person singular ending of the perfect active indicative (basically equivalent to the Spanish preterite) of the first conjugation verbs (§58a): CL *laudāvit* > VL *laudaut* (Sp. loó), CL *cantāvit* > *cantaut* (Sp. cantó). This phenomenon is doubly unusual because it is one of the rare cases when a final Classical Latin vowel was not retained in Vulgar Latin.

§6. There was one case of a vowel appearing in Vulgar Latin where there had been none in Classical Latin. An *i-*, later to become *e-* in Western Romance through normal phonetic evolution, began to appear at the beginning of a word that began with *s* + *consonant*. The earliest known example dates from 79 A.D. in Pompeii: CL *Smyrna* > VL *Ismurna*; it was the name of a local prostitute scrawled on the ouside of the brothel. There are many other attested examples from other parts of the Roman Empire showing more common words: CL *schola* > VL *iscola* (Sp. escuela), CL *statuam* > VL *istatua* (Sp. estatua), CL *scrīptam* > VL *iscripta* (Sp. escrita).

Why did this change come about? The reason is that in all other cases where there was an *s* + *consonant* in Latin, the *s* ended the preceding syllable: *pas-tor* 'shepherd', *aus-cul-ta-re* 'to listen', *do-mes-ti-cus* 'domestic'. The addition of the *i-* (called a PROTHETIC vowel by philologists) must have been initiated in order to regularize the sound system, allowing the *s* to end a syllable, as is usually did when a consonant followed. Vulgar Latin speakers did not tolerate seeming irregularities, and they endeavored to 'correct' them, as in this case.

§7a. In Classical Latin, if an *e* was in HIATUS with another vowel (that is, if an *e* was in contact with another vowel), each vowel counted as a separate syllable: *vī-ne-a* (Sp. viña) had three syllables, as did *lan-ce-a* (Sp. lanza) and *ca-ve-a* 'cage'. In Vulgar Latin, these *e*'s turned into the SEMI-VOWEL[8] [y] and the result of

---

[8] A pure VOWEL is a sound produced with tongue and mouth in a stationary potition; a SEMI-VOWEL is produced with the organs of speech moving; these semi-vowels are often called GLIDES—a very descriptive term, for

the process was that the words lost a syllable as the semi-vowel merged with the following vowel to form a single syllable: VL *vinia* [vi-nya], *lancia* [lan-tsya], *cavia* [ca-vya]. The three examples cited above are from the *Appendix Probi*:

> vīnea non vinia
> lancea non lancia
> cavea non cavia

One also sees at Pompeii the two syllable *abiat* [a-byat] for the three syllable *habeat* [a-be-at].

The creation of the semi-vowel [y], which is known as YOD (after the Hebrew vowel of the same name), was to bring about some far-reaching changes in both the Spanish vocalic and consonantal systems. In the history of Spanish, there developed a number of types of yods; this one was the earliest.

b. If a stressed *e* or *i* was in hiatus, one of two things happened. In a short word, the stressed vowel was raised, as in these attested examples:

> CL mĕa > VL mia
> CL vĭa > VL via

Ordinarily, of course, the CL ĕ becomes ę in Vulgar Latin, and not *i*, and the CL ĭ becomes Vulgar Latin ę.

c. In longer words, the stress moved to the more open of the vowels. This phenomenon produced a yod as the stress changed place:

> CL mulíerem > VL muliére (Sp. mujer)
> CL lintéolum > VL lintiólu (Sp. lenzuelo)
> CL paríetem > VL pariéte > paréte (Sp. pared)

In the last example, the yod of *parete* seems to have been swallowed up in the course of its development by the *r*, giving the attested VL *parete*.

§8. In hiatus, like vowels contracted:

> CL lībrariī 'copiers' > VL librari
> CL lignariī 'carpenters' > VL lignari
> CL mortuus (Sp. muerto) > VL mortus

---

one's tongue does glide from one vowel position to another when producing a semi-vowel.

> CL ingenuus 'natural' > VL ingenus
> CL carduus 'thistle' > VL cardus

The fourth century grammarian Charisius commented "*Carduus trium syllabarum est*" '*Cardus* is of three syllables,' thus indicating that *cardus* (with only two syllables), 'incorrect' in the Classical language, appears to have been the form in current use in Charisius' time.

§9. Finally, a characteristic of the Western Vulgar Latin vocalic system that was to have a great effect on the development of Spanish consonants was that the unstressed vowels in the middle of words began to fall. This falling of vowels is known as SYNCOPATION, and there are a number of examples of this feature in the *Appendix Probi*:

> speculum non speclum (Sp. espejo)
> masculus non masclus (Sp. macho)
> vetulus non veclus (Sp. viejo)
> articulus non articlus (Sp. artejo)
> oculus non oclus (Sp. ojo)

a. As the vowel fell, its absence sometimes created consonant clusters that had been unknown in the middle of Latin words, such as *-scl-* and *-cl-*. As Vulgar Latin developed, it had to cope with the new consonant clusters as well as it could; the Spanish results indicate that the clusters had to pass through a number of stages before they became phonetically stable. It should be said that the fall of the vowel in CL *vetulus* 'should have' given VL *vetlus*, but since the *-tl-* cluster was so foreign to Latin, it quickly changed to the *-cl-* cluster, which was fast becoming common.

b. Many times after syncopation, the resulting consonant cluster was one that had already existed in Classical Latin and it offered no phonetic complications:

> CL aridus 'arid' > VL ardus
> CL solidus (Sp. sueldo) > VL soldus
> CL viridis (Sp. verde) > VL virdis
> CL positus (Sp. puesto) > VL postus

The Vulgar Latin Consonantal System

§10. A development which was to have far-reaching effect on Vulgar Latin grammar was the universal loss of final *m* on words longer than one syllable; this phenomenon dates from the third century B.C. Here are some examples from the *Appendix Probi*:

> pridem non pride 'some time ago'
> olim non oli 'formerly'
> idem non ide 'the same'
> numquam non nunqua (Sp. nunca)

Just how the loss of final *m* affected Vulgar Latin grammar will be seen in §24.

In monosyllabic words, the final *m* generally was preserved throughout Vulgar Latin: CL *quem* > VL *quem* (Sp. quien), CL *cum* > VL *cum* (Sp. con), CL *tam* > VL *tam* (Sp. tan), CL *rem* > VL *rem* (OSp. ren 'thing').

§11a. Another phonetic feature of Western Vulgar Latin was the change of *p*, *t*, and the *k* sound to *b*, *d*, and *g* when between vowels (that is in INTERVOCALIC position) or when between a vowel and *r*. This process, known as VOICING, is illustrated in these examples attested in inscriptions:

> CL trī*t*icum > VL tri*d*icum (Sp. trigo)
> CL lo*c*us > VL logus (Sp. luego)
> CL inmu*t*avit > VL inmu*d*avit 'he changed'
> CL pū*t*orem > VL pu*d*ore (Sp. pudor)
> CL le*p*ra > VL le*b*ra 'leprosy'
> CL fri*c*āre > VL fregare (Sp. fregar)
> CL mī*c*at > VL migat 'he trembles'

b. If *p*, *t*, and *k* evolved to *b*, *d* and *g* in Vulgar Latin, the question must arise: just what happened to Classical Latin *b*, *d*, and *g* between vowels? Although the *b* remained strong, as time passed, Classical *d* and *g* tended to fall; in fact, even in Vulgar Latin the intervocalic *g* had changed to a yod and had already begun to fall, especially before *i*:

> CL magister > VL maester 'teacher'
> CL rēgīna > VL reína (Sp. reina)
> CL magis > VL mais (Sp. más)
> CL vīgintī > VL viinti (Sp. veinte)
> CL trīgintī > VL triinta (Sp. treinta)

§12. The Classical Latin *v* was originally a semi-vowel pronounced [w]; *vīvō* was pronounced [wíwo] and *vīnum* was pronounced [wínum]. Among other proofs, this fact is borne out by

Greek transliterations of Latin words. The name of the Roman Emperor Nerva (32-98 A.D.) was transliterated Νερουασ [néruas]. The man's name Valerius was transliterated Ουαλεριοσ [ualérios], and the volcano Vesuvius was Ουεσυιον [uɛsúion]. After the first century of our era, however, we find the Classical *v* transliterated with a beta [β = b]: Nerva > Νερβασ [nérbas], Vesuvius > Βεσβιον [bɛsbion].

In Vulgar Latin, it was this [b] that became the standard pronunciation for both Vulgar Latin *b* and *v*, thus causing the one to be hopelessly confused with the other in spelling. Our Roman schoolteacher tried in vain to correct this confusion in the *Appendix Probi*:

> baclus non vaclus 'cane'
> vapulo non baplo 'I am beaten'
> plebes non plevis 'plebeian class'

Additional examples are found in 'Classical Latin' inscriptions carved by people who were only semi-literate: CL *ūniversis* > VL *unibersis*, CL *cīvitātis* > VL *cibitatis* of a city', CL *vīxit* > VL *bixit* 'he lived'.

§13. In Classical Latin, the *c* was pronounced [k] before all vowels. Our modern notion that the Classical *c* was pronounced [č] before *e* and *i* derives from the way it came to be pronounced, through normal phonetic development, at the time of the Carolinigian Renaissance (ca. 800 A.D.) when vigorous efforts were made to restore Classical Latin as a *lingua franca*; this pronunciation has been with us ever since.

There are a number of proofs, however, which clearly show that the Classical *c* was pronounced [k]. In the Logudurese dialect of Sardinian, recognized as the phonetically least developed of any Romance dialect, the [k] has been preserved before *e* and *i*: CL *cerbum* 'deer' > Log. *kerbu*; CL *cēram* 'wax' > Log. *kera*; Late Latin *circare* 'go across' > Log. *kircare*; CL *caelum* 'sky' > Log. *kelu*.

Some Classical Latin words were borrowed by Old Germanic during the time of the Roman Empire, and they still preserve the ancient [k] in modern German: CL *cellārium* 'cellar' > Germ. *Keller*; CL *ceraseam* > Germ. *Kirsch* 'cherry'; CL *Caesar* > Germ. *Kaiser*.

The Romans conquered the Iberian Peninsula in about 197 B.C., and, from the earliest days, Latin loanwords went into Basque, the pre-Roman language of the northern part of the peninsula. CL *pacem* 'peace' > Basque *bake* was one of the early loanwords; the

[k] is still preserved.

In Vulgar Latin, the *c* remained [k] before a mid- or back-vowel, but before a front vowel it PALATALIZED (that is, it came to be pronounced against the roof of the mouth, the 'palate') and became the sound [ts]. The evolution seems to have been this: *centu* [kéntu] > [kyéntu] > [tyéntu] > [tséntu].

a. As the third and fourth stages of the above series indicate, *t* + *yod* also yielded the sound [ts] in Vulgar Latin. There are inscriptions from the third century with spelling errors because of the confusion between *ti* and *ci*, both of which were pronounced the same way: *terminaciones* for *terminationes*, *definiciones* for *definitiones*, and *terciae* for *tertiae*. A Vulgar Latin word which passed into Germanic, probably in the fifth century A.D., also confirms the [ts] pronunciation. Germ. *Zins* [tsins] from CL *census* 'census'.

b. The *qu* cluster, which had been pronounced [kw] in all cases in Classical Latin, simplified to [k] before all vowels (except *a*) in Vulgar Latin:

> CL sequī [sékwi] > VL sequire [sekíre] (Sp. seguir)
> CL quem [kwɛm] > VL quem [kɛm] (Sp. quien)
> CL quiētum [kwiétum] > VL quetu [kétu] 'quiet'
> CL quōmodo [kwómodo] > VL comodo [kómodo] (Sp. como)

When did [kw] simplify to [k]? It must have been only *after* the Latin [k] had changed to [ts] before *e* and *i*, otherwise the Spanish result of the first two examples would have been the non-existent *secir* and *cen*.

There is one example, however, where *qu* before *i* did become [ts]. CL *quīnque* [kwíŋkwe] gave VL *cinque* [tsíŋke] (Sp. cinco) through the loss of the first *u* by DISSIMILATION (§149). That is, since a language sometimes may not allow two like sounds in the same word (and this is certainly true in the case of Spanish), one of the sounds may be changed in some way, or even eliminated, as it is here, where *kw - kw* changed to *k - kw*, and early enough for the first *k* to evolve to [ts].

c. Before *a*, the [kw] usually remained intact: CL *quando* [kwándo] > VL [kwándo] (Sp. cuando).

§14. The *h* sound had disappeared very early, even before Classical Latin had become a literary language, although the *h* remained in Classical Latin spelling. In Vulgar Latin, since no *h* was pronounced, none was written. At Pompeii, *abiat* was written for *habeat* (Sp. haya has a restored *h*), *anc* for *hanc* 'this', *omo* for *homo* 'man', *ora* for *hora* (Sp. hora, again with a restored *h*). The *Appendix Probi* gives this orthographic admonition:

> hostiae non ostiae 'victims'
> adhuc non aduc 'until now'

§15. In Vulgar Latin, a number of consonant clusters simplified. Here are some attested examples:

a. ns > s

> a*ns*a non a*s*a (Sp. asa) [*Appendix Probi*]
> me*ns*a non me*s*a (Sp. mesa) [*Appendix Probi*]
> CL co*ns*iderate > VL cosiderate 'consider'
> CL mo*ns*trat > VL mostrat (Sp. muestra)
> CL Romane*ns*es > VL Romaneses 'Romans'
> CL spo*ns*ae > VL ispo*s*e 'spouse'

Since *-ns-* simplified quite early to *-s-*, old and modern Spanish words with *-ns-* show themselves to be borrowings directly from Classical Latin; *pensar* and *consentir* are examples of these.

b. ps > ss

> CL ipse > VL isse (Sp. ese)
> CL ipsam > VL issa (Sp. esa)
> CL scrīpsit > VL scrisset 'he wrote'

c. pt > tt

> CL septem > VL sette (Sp. siete)

d. rs > ss

> CL dorsum > VL dossu 'back'
> CL ursum > VL ussu (Sp. oso)
> CL sursum > VL susu (OSp. suso)
> CL persona > VL pessona 'person'

Sp. *persona* is a learned word.

e. nct > nt

> CL cinctus > VL cintus 'cinched'
> CL defunctus > VL defuntus 'dead'
> CL sanctum > VL santu (Sp. santo)

f. mn > nn

> CL alumnus > VL alunnus 'student'
> CL damnum > VL dannu (Sp. daño)

Sp. *alumno* is obviously a learned word.

g. gr > r

> CL integrum > VL interu (Sp. entero)
> CL pigritia > VL piritia (Sp. pereza)

Vulgar Latin Stress

§16. In order to understand Vulgar Latin stress patterns, a few comments first need to be made about Classical Latin stress. If a Classical Latin word had only one syllable, it was stressed on that syllable:

> měl (Sp. miel)
> ŏs 'mouth'
> nŏx 'night'
> mūs 'mouse'

A word that is stressed on the last syllable (= ultima) is called OXY-TONIC. In Classical Latin there are no oxytonic words except for the monosyllabics.

If a word has two syllables, it is stressed on the first at all times:

> ěmō 'I buy'
> cănĭs 'dog'
> ěrrăt 'he wanders'
> hŏra (Sp. hora)

Philologists use PAROXYTONIC to mean 'stressed on the next-to-last syllable' (= penult). A great percentage of Classical Latin words are paroxytonic.

If a word has more than two syllables in it, it can be paroxytonic or PROPAROXYTONIC, that is, 'stressed on the second-from-last syllable' (= antepenult) according to this simple rule: if the next-to-last syllable contains a long vowel, the word is paroxytonic; it if contains a short vowel, the word is proparoxytonic:

Proparoxytonic Stress	Paroxytonic Stress
natūra 'nature'	sátira 'satire'
servíle (Sp. servil)	fácĭlis (Sp. fácil)
convēnit 'he met'	cónvĕnit 'he meets'
extrēmus 'extreme'	líbĕrī 'children'

There is one variation of this rule. A short syllable is *considered* long for purposes of stress if a consonant ends the syllable. Philologists call the syllable LONG BY POSITION in this circumstance, even if its vowel is short, as these examples show:

> extĕrnus (ex-tĕr-nus) 'foreign'
> invĭctus (in-vĭc-tus) 'unconquered'
> contĭngit (con-tĭn-git) 'it touches'
> tempĕstas (tem-pĕs-tas) 'storm'

§17. The general rule is that the Classical Latin stressed vowel remained as the Vulgar Latin stressed vowel, even if there was syncopation: CL *vírĭdis* > VL *vírdis*, CL *ócŭlus* > VL *óclus*.

a. There were, however, three cases where the stress *did* change place in Vulgar Latin. The first instance has already been seen in a section dealing with hiatus (§7c): CL *paríetem* > VL *paríéte*, CL *lintéolum* > VL *lintiólu*.

b. The second stress change affected a number of verbs with prefixes. Before showing the stress change, it is important to set down a few comments about the effect of prefixes. In Classical Latin, if a prefix was attached to a verb (or noun or adjective, for that matter), the prefix usually had a phonetic effect on the stem vowel of the verb, raising its point of articulation:

> tángō 'I touch'; contíngō 'I find'
> fáciō 'I make'; perfíciō 'I finish'
> cláudō 'I close'; inclūdō 'I include'

If the rules permitted, the stress could shift to the prefix:

> cádō 'I fall'; 'I fall down'
> tĕnet 'he holds'; rétĭnet 'he retains'
> prĕmō 'I press'; cómprĭmō 'I compress'

Now, here is where the stress change took place; if Vulgar Latin speakers recognized that the verb was a compound, the *original* stem vowel was restored and the accent shifted back to the stem of the verb:

> CL récipit > VL recípit (Sp. recibe)
> CL cóntinet > VL conténet (Sp. contiene)
> CL rétinet > VL reténet (Sp. retiene)
> CL cónvenit > VL convénit (Sp. conviene)

But if the verb was *not* recognized as a compound, the stress remained where it had been in Classical Latin: CL *cóllocat* (= cum + locat) > VL *cóllocat* (Sp. cuelga); CL *cómputat* (= cum + putat) > VL *cómputo* (Sp. cuento). Needless to say, the Spanish *coloco* and *computo* are learned words.

c. The third shift in stress did not affect many words. If a proparoxytonic word had a *stop + r* in the last syllable, the stress was attracted to the next-to-last syllable. (A STOP is a sound produced first by stopping and then releasing the air from within the mouth; examples include [p, t, k, b, d, g].) This phenomenon is quite easy to grasp through the examples below:

> CL íntegrum > VL intégru (Sp. entero)
> CL cáthedra > VL catédra (Sp. cadera)
> CL cólubra > VL colúbra (Sp. culebra)
> CL ténebras > VL tenébras (Sp. tinieblas)

The Vulgar Latin Declension System

§18. In order to understand the Vulgar Latin DECLENSIONS (that is, the systems used to show grammatical functions of nouns and adjectives) it is first necessary to speak about the Classical declensions. From Indo-European linguistic stock, Classical Latin inherited three genders, a wealth of grammatical endings, and five different declension groups.

The three classical genders were MASCULINE, FEMININE, and NEUTER. Except for male and female beings (*hōmo, m* 'man' and *mulier, f* 'woman', for example), the genders were arbitrarily distributed, as the examples below show:

masculine	*feminine*	*neuter*
pēs 'foot'	manus 'hand'	caput 'head'
sūcus 'juice'	aqua 'water'	lāc 'milk'
panis 'bread'	mēnsa 'table'	vīnum 'wine'

In Classical Latin, suffixes attached to nouns told their grammatical function. There were six suffixes for the singular and six for the plural. As example of the various possibilities, the declension of *amīcus, m* 'friend' is given below:

	Singular	Plural
nominative	amīcus	amīcī
genitive	amīcī	amīcōrum
dative	amīcō	amīcīs
accusative	amīcum	amīcōs
ablative	amīcō	amīcīs
vocative	amīce	amīcī

The NOMINATIVE case indicates that the noun is the subject of the sentence: *Amīcus est hīc* 'A friend is here.' The GENITIVE case means that the noun possesses (something): *Dōmus amīcī* 'The house of a friend.' The DATIVE case means that the noun is the indirect object: *Dō panem amīcō* 'I give bread to a friend.' The ACCUSATIVE case means that the noun is the direct object: *Videō amīcum* 'I see a friend.' The ABLATIVE case has a number of functions; one of its a very common uses is as the object of a preposition: *Vadō cum amīcō* 'I go with a friend'. The VOCATIVE case is used in direct address: *O, amīce!* 'Oh, friend!'

§19. Classical Latin nouns fall broadly into five declensions. The first declension is composed almost exclusively of feminine nouns and is characterized by an -*a*- in most of its endings. There are a great number of first declension nouns.

puella, -ae[9] *f* 'girl'

nom.	puella	puellae
gen.	puellae	puellārum
dat.	puellae	puellīs
acc.	puellam	puellas
abl.	puellā	puellīs

The vocative case in all declensions but the second is exactly like the nominative form. The function of those forms that are spelled the same becomes apparent in context.

---

[9] In Latin grammars and dictionaries, the genitive singular endings of nouns is listed with the nominative singular: *puella, -ae*. This is particularly useful since the genitive is the most useful form to help us distinguish which declension the noun belongs to, especially for the third declension, all of which will be seen later.

§20. The second declension is comprised of masculine and neuter nouns, and is characterized by the endings given below. There are a great number of second declension nouns as well.

	servus, -ī m 'slave'		*dōnum, -ī n* 'gift'	
	singular	*plural*	*singular*	*plural*
nom.	servus	servī	dōnum	dōna
gen.	servī	servōrum	dōnī	dōnōrum
dat.	servō	servīs	dōnō	dōnīs
acc.	servum	servōs	dōnum	dōna
abl.	servō	servīs	dōnō	donīs
voc.	serve	servī	dōnum	dona

A few masculine second declension nouns, such as *puer, -ī, m* 'boy' have no *-us* in the nominative singular, but otherwise they follow the pattern regularly.

It should be noticed that the neuter nouns here, and always, in all declensions, show the same form in the accusative that they show in the nominative within each number.

§21. The third declension has masculine, feminine, and neuter nouns, and is more complicated than the first two declensions. Its complexity arises from four causes. First, the gender of the nouns is not automatic as it almost always is in the first two declensions. Second, there are several sets of case endings for this declension. Third, the stressed syllable sometimes varies among the singular forms of the declension (the stress stays in the same place throughout the first and second declension singulars). Rules for Classical Latin stress explain why this is so (§16). Fourth, the nominative singular almost always has one syllable less than the remaining four forms of the singular. Linguists call this type of declension IMPARISYLLABIC. (If the number of syllables remains constant throughout the singular, the declension is PARISYLLABIC.) The third declension, like the first and second, also comprises a great number of nouns.

a. Here are some examples of the imparisyllabic third declension nouns. The first example (*rēx*) shows no shift in stress, but the second example (*cīvitās*) does. The third example (*corpus*), a neuter, is given to show the neuter endings; its nominative and accusative are characteristically the same in each number.

rḗx, rḗgis, m 'king'   cívitas, cīvitā́tis, f 'state'

nom.	rḗx	rḗges	cívitās	cīvitā́tes
gen.	rḗgis	rḗgum	cīvitā́tis	cīvitā́tum
dat.	rḗgī	rḗgibus	cīvitā́ti	cīvitā́tibus
acc.	rḗgem	rḗges	cīvitā́tem	cīvitā́tes
abl.	rḗge	rḗgibus	cīvitā́te	cīvitā́tibus

córpus, córporis, n 'body'

nom.	córpus	córpora
gen.	córporis	córporum
dat.	córporī	corpóribus
acc.	córpus	córpora
abl.	córpore	corpóribus

b. Finally, here are two parisyllabic examples, among the few in the third declension:

nū́bēs,-is f 'cloud'   máre, -is n 'sea'

nom.	nū́bēs	nū́bēs	máre	mária
gen.	nū́bis	nū́bium	máris	márium
dat.	nū́bī	nū́bibus	márī	máribus
acc.	nū́bēs	nū́bēs	máre	mária
abl.	nū́be	nū́bibus	márī	máribus

These particular examples illustrate yet another complication of the third declension: the genitive plural of both examples ends in -ium (instead of -um, as in other third declension nouns). Examples such as nū́bēs and mare are known as 'i-stem' third declension nouns becasue of the i which ends the stem of the genitive plural.

§22. The fourth declension had only a few nouns, mostly feminine, and was characterized by a u in most endings. Masculine and feminine nouns of this declension shared the same set of endings, but the neuters had a set of their own:

mánus, -ūs f 'hand'   córnu, -ūs n 'horn'

nom.	mánus	mánūs	córnu	córnua
gen.	mánūs	mánuum	córnūs	córnuum
dat.	mánuī	mánibus	córnū	córnibus
acc.	mánum	mánūs	córnū	córnua
abl.	mánū	mánibus	córnū	córnibus

Other common words of this declension include *dómus, -ūs f* 'house'; some kinship terms: *sócrus, -ūs f* 'mother-in-law', *nŭrus, -ūs f* 'daughter-in-law'; the word for 'fruit': *frúctus, -ūs m*; and the names of some trees, all of which are feminine: *pĭnus, -ūs,* 'pine'; *fráxinus, -ūs,* 'ash tree'; *fĭcus, -ūs,* 'fig tree'.

§23. The fifth declension comprised very few nouns, and was characterized by the letter *e* throughout the endings. All nouns of this declension were feminine, except *dĭes, -ēī,* 'day' which could be either masculine or feminine. An odd feature of this declension is that only two nouns (*dĭes, -ēī* and *rēs, ĕī* 'thing') had plural forms; the rest were declined only in the singular.

	dĭes, -ēī m + f 'day'		*mātériēs, -ēī f* 'material'
nom.	díēs	díēs	mātériēs
gen.	diéī	diérum	māteriéī
dat.	diéī	diébus	māteriéī
acc	díem	díēs	mātériem
abl.	díē	diébus	mātériē

Some other nouns of this declension are *fĭdēs, -ēī* f 'faith', and *spēs, -ēī* f 'hope'.

§24. Vulgar Latin nouns were organized quite differently from Classical Latin nouns. First, of the five main cases of Classical Latin, only *two* (the nominative and the accusative) were used in Vulgar Latin. Second, only the first three Classical Latin declensions were continued in Vulgar Latin, and, third, the neuter gender disappeared in Vulgar Latin.

There seem to be two related reasons why the five Classical Latin cases were reduced to two. The first reason is that the endings would have become hopelessly confused through normal phonetic evolution in Vulgar Latin (§§4, 5, 10); the singular examples below show how the neat grammatical system based on endings would have been destroyed if all cases had been maintained in Vulgar Latin. The genitive, dative and ablative examples below *never* existed, and are given only for purposes of the demonstration. It also should be noticed that the transcription has been made as the sounds would have been pronounced (in inscriptions, Vulgar Latin carvers maintained the final *u* even tough they pronounced it *o*).

	First Declension		*Second Declension*	
	Classical Latin	*Vulgar Latin*	*Classical Latin*	*Vulgar Latin*
nom.	puella	puella	servus	servos
gen.	puellae	puelle	servī	servi
dat.	puellae	puelle	servō	servo
acc.	puellam	puella	servum	servo
abl.	puellā	puella	servō	servo

In the first declension, the four distinct forms would have been reduced to only two, and the nominative, accusative, and ablative, once distinct from each other, would now be confused. In the second declension, the five different forms would have been reduced to three. This time, the dative, accusative, and ablative would have been mixed together.

§25. One would think that because of the latent phonetic confusion of the case endings, Vulgar Latin would not have been able to distinguish grammatical functions any longer, but such was not the case at all. The system that Vulgar Latin used to differentiate grammatical functions is the second reason for the reduction of cases, but in order to explain this second reason, the differences between SYNTHETIC and ANALYTIC language must be given. A synthetic language, like Classical Latin, is one in which grammatical information is attached to the end of words (*serv-ī* = of the slave), and an analytic language, like Vulgar Latin, English, and French, is one where grammatical information precedes the words, or is inferred from syntactic position.

§26. At the outset, Vulgar Latin showed itself to be an analytic language in nouns, adjectives and verbs. In the noun declension system, Vulgar Latin largely retained the nominative (one of the two most common cases) in the nominative function, i.e., as the subject of a sentence. It also kept the accusative (the other of the two most common cases) in a variety of functions. The Vulgar Latin accusative, aside from its use as a direct object, was also used following certain prepositions to replace analytically the other Classical cases: *de* + *accusative* replaced the Classical genitive case; *ad* + *accusative* replaced the Classical dative case; and any of the other usual prepositions + *accusative* replaced the *preposition* + *ablative* use of Classical Latin.

There are two questions that arise from the reasoning above: did the phonetic confusion cause Vulgar Latin to become an analytic language? or would Vulgar Latin have been analytic in its structure even if there had been no phonetically confused forms? Evidence seems to favor an affirmative answer to the second part of the question.

§27. The first declension in Vulgar Latin looked like this:

porta 'door'

	Singular	Plural
nom.	porta	porte (portas)
acc.	porta	portas

Due to normal phonetic development, the singular forms shared the same spelling in the first declension (§10). In the plural, *porte* is the normal phonetic development from CL *portae*, yet there was alternate nominative plural (*portas*) based on the *accusative* plural form. In Vulgar Latin, since the accusative had taken over the functions of the four OBLIQUE cases (i.e., all of the cases except the nominative), it began to encroach on the territory of the nominative as well. The accusative takeover of the nominative function is shown in this famous, and often misunderstood gravestone inscription found in the *Corpus Inscriptionum Latinarum*, iii, 3351:

Hic quescunt duas matres, duas filias; numero tres facunt

"Here lie two mothers and two daughters; that makes three." Students of Classical Latin would expect to see *duae filiae* since the two daughters are part of the subject of the sentence, but the accusative form has taken over the nominative here. The third declension nominative plural, *matres*, with its final -*s*, provides a springboard for the analogy.

Many people think that the two mothers plus the two daughters must equal *four* persons, and not three. But on reflection they will see that the point of the inscription is that there is a grandmother, her daughter and her granddaughter all buried together: two mothers and two daughters, that makes three.

§28a. The second declension masculines passed easily into Vulgar Latin, but the neuters suffered some changes. Below is a typical development of a masculine noun in Vulgar Latin. Again, the words are transcribed as they would have been pronounced, rather than the way they would have been carved:

amicos 'friend'

	Singular	Plural
nom.	amicos	amici
acc.	amico	amicos

The nominative singular and the accusative plural developed to the same form, unlike the corresponding Classical Latin forms, which were different (*amīcus, amīcōs*); this fact certainly contributed to the eventual universal takeover of the nominative function by the accusative.

b. The neuters of the second declension showed two types of changes. Those that usually were used in the singular changed to masculine because of the similarity of form:

> CL collum > VL collus (Sp. cuello)
> CL nasum > VL nasus 'nose'
> CL vīnum > VL vinus (Sp. vino)

c. On the other hand, those that were commonly seen in the plural changed to the first declension (feminine) singular since the -*a* of the neuter plural (§20) was easily confused with the first singular:

CL 2nd decl.	VL 1st decl. fem.
Neuter pl.	*Singular*
pirum, *pl.*pira	pira (Sp. pera)
festum, *pl.* festa	festa (Sp. fiesta)
folium, *pl.* folia	folia (Sp. hoja)
lignum, *pl.* ligna	ligna (Sp. leña)
signum, *pl.* signa	signa (Sp. seña)

The *Appendix Probi* shows a correction of a neuter plural mistaken for a feminine singular: *vico castrorum non vico castrae. Castra* was a neuter plural having the singular meaning 'camp', so 'of the camp' was "rationally" rendered by the genitive *singular* of the first declension. (*Vico* referred to 'town'.)

§29. The third declension had inherited some built-in complications from Classical Latin, and was due to suffer a number of changes in Vulgar Latin.

a. Since its case endings were the same for both masculine and feminine nouns, some third declension nouns changed gender in

Vulgar Latin. Here are examples of Classical masculine nouns that became feminine in the Vulgar Latin of Hispania:

	Masculine		*Feminine*
CL	frontem	VL	fronte (Sp. frente)
CL	fontem	VL	fonte (Sp. fuente)
CL	parietem	VL	parete (Sp. pared)
CL	serpentem	VL	serpente (Sp. serpiente)

b. Third declension neuters became masculine or feminine in the Vulgar Latin of Hispania, but, as the examples from the modern Romance Languages show, the same preference was not maintained in other areas where Vulgar Latin was spoken. (The Portuguese article *o* shown in the examples is masculine):

	Neuter		*Masculine or Feminine*
CL	mare	VL	mare (Sp. *el mar*, Ptg. *o mar*, Fr. *la mer*)
CL	salem	VL	sale (Sp. *la sal*, Ptg. *o sal*, Fr. *le sel*)
CL	lac	VL	lacte (Sp. *la leche*, Ptg. *o leite*, Fr. *le lait*)
CL	mel	VL	mele (Sp. *la miel*, Ptg. *o mel*, Fr. *la miel*)

VL *lacte* was rebuilt on the genitive stem *lact-*.

An inscription in Pompeii shows that the neuter *cadaver* had become masculine since the following adjective was also masculine: *cadaver mortuus*.

c. One third declension neuter, *opus*, pl. *opera*, had a first declension doublet already in Classical Latin where *opera*, the nominative plural of the original form, was used as a new nominative singular. *Opera* was continued as a feminine throughout Romance and gave *la obra* in Spanish.

§30. There were two tendencies in the third declension imparisyllabic nouns. Those without a moveable stress (§21a) added a syllable to the nominative (usually making it exactly like the genitive in form) to make the declension even out to fit a parisyllabic pattern. This was a device used to 'regularize' Vulgar Latin.

	Classical Latin	*Vulgar Latin*
nom.	mons 'mountain'	móntis
acc.	móntem	mónte
nom.	bos 'ox'	bóvis
acc.	bóvem	bóve

The *Appendix Probi* 'corrected' some of these rebuilt nominatives: *grus non gruis* 'stork', *pectin non pectinis* 'comb', *glis non gliris* 'dormouse'.

The moveable stress imparisyllabics (§21a) retained the original nominative form:

	Classical Latin	Vulgar Latin
nom.	sérmo 'speech'	sérmo
acc.	sermónem	sermóne
nom.	dólor 'pain'	dólor
acc.	dolórem	dolóre
nom.	rátio 'calculation'	rátio
acc.	ratiónem	ratióne

Typical Vulgar Latin third declension nouns would look like this, then:

	Non-moveable stress		Moveable stress	
	Singular	Plural	Singular	Plural
nom.	móntis	móntes	dólor	dolóres
acc.	mónte	móntes	dolóre	dolóres

§31. The fourth declension disappeared completely, and its forms were assimilated almost entirely by the second declension, with which it has similarities in form. Most of the words that made this particular move were either neuter or feminine, but the switch made them almost exclusively masculine:

Classical Latin Fourth Declension	Vulgar Latin Second Declension
cornu, *n*	cornus (Sp. cuerno)
gelu, *n*	gelus (Sp. hielo)
genu, *n*	genus 'knee'
caput, *n*	capus 'head'
fraxinus, *f*	fraxinus, *m* (Sp. fresno)
pīnus, *f*	pinus, *m* (Sp. pino)
manus, *f*	manus, *f* (Sp. la mano)

Two fourth declension words, the names of female beings, were virtually forced to the first declension, and both are documented in the *Appendix Probi*:

nurus non nura (Sp. nuera)
socrus non socra (Sp. suegra)

§32. The few words of the fifth declension were assimilated
into the first and third declensions. Already in Classical Latin a
number of fifth declension nouns had doublets in the first declension: CL 5th decl. *materiēs*, 1st decl. *materia*; CL 5th decl. *luxuriēs*,
1st decl. *luxuria*. Because of the influence of the doublets, the way
was paved for most of the fifth declension to move to the first.
Similarities between the nominatives and accusatives of the fifth
and third declensions caused the remaining nouns to move to the
third declension.

Classical Latin *Fifth Declension*	*Vulgar Latin* *First or Third Declension*
materiēs	materia, 1st decl. (Sp. madera)
diēs, *m*	dia, 1st decl. (Sp. el día)
rabiēs	rabia, (Sp. rabia)
saniēs	sania, 1st decl. (Sp. saña)
faciēs	facia, 3rd. decl. (Sp. haz)
fidēs	fides, 3rd. decl. (Sp. fe)

§33. Vulgar Latin, unlike Classical Latin, was partial to nouns
with diminutive endings even when the result connoted no diminutive meaning. This predilection is due to a number of reasons:
a. Since Vulgar Latin tried to be very expressive, it made
nouns more expressive by adding diminutive suffixes.

CL neptis > VL nepticula 'granddaughter'
CL culter > VL cultellus 'knife'
CL agnus > VL agnellus 'lamb'

b. Adding a diminutive suffix to a noun was an easy way to
change the gender of neuters since these were either masculine or
feminine, and never neuter:

CL auris, *n* > VL oricla, *f* (Sp. oreja)
CL genu, *n* > VL genuculu, *m* (Sp. hinojo)
CL caput, *m* > VL capitia, *f* (Sp. cabeza)

c. Vulgar Latin did not favor very short words; the addition of
a dimunitive suffix added one or two new syllables to make any
short word acceptable in length:

CL acus > VL acucula (Sp. aguja)
CL avus > VL aviolu (Sp. abuelo)
CL apis > VL apicula (Sp. abeja)
CL caepa > VL cepulla (Sp. cebolla)
CL ovis > VL ovicula (Sp. oveja)

§34. Classical Latin, unlike Classical Greek, had no definite or indefinite articles, and according to Quintilian, did not want any: *"Noster sermo articulōs non desiderat."* 'Our language does not want articles." *Inst. Ora.*, I, 4, 9. But Vulgar Latin, with its need for expressiveness and clarity, began to use the weakened Classical demonstratives *illum* and *illam* for the definite articles in Hispania, and the numerals *ūnum* and *ūnam* for the indefinite articles.

Adjective Declensions

§35a. Classical Latin adjectives agreed in gender, number and case with the nouns they modified. There were two types of adjectives. The first type used the endings of the first and second declensions; the first declension endings being used when modifying feminine nouns and the second declension endings when modifying masculine nouns, and the neuter variants for neuter nouns. In grammar books, this type of adjective is identified with the nominative singular ending of all three genders: *bonus, -a, -um* 'good'.

b. The second type of adjective used third declension 'i-stem' endings (§21b). It showed the same endings when modifying masculine and feminine nouns (since the correspnding noun declension made no formal masculine or feminine distinction either), but in the neuter had a different form shared by the nominative and accusative. In grammar books, this adjective is identified in this way: *fortis, -e* 'strong'. The main entry is the masculine/feminine nominative singular form, and the alternate ending indicates the neuter form.

Vulgar Latin (and the Romance Languages) retained both types of adjectives, but, of course, the neuter form disappeared in Vulgar Latin (and therefore in Romance as well), as did all cases except the nominative and accusative.

c. In a few instances, some adjectives based on the third declension tried to move to the first/second declension type, but with extremely limited ultimate success, as these examples from the *Appendix Probi* show:

tristis non tristus (Sp. triste)
pauper mulier non paupera mulier (Sp. pobre [mujer])
acer non acrum 'sour'

Typical examples of Vulgar Latin adjectives would look like this:

bellus, -a 'pretty'   *fortis,* 'strong'

nom.	bellus, -a	belli, -ae	fortis	fortes
acc.	bellu, -a	bellos, -as	forte	fortes

§36. The comparative and superlative degrees of adjectives were synthetic forms in Classical Latin; that is, the comparative or superlative aspect of the adjective was suffixed onto the adjective.

a. In the comparative degree, all Classical Latin adjectives had endings based on the ordinary (not the 'i-stem') third declension (§21a). This meant that an adjective of the first type (based on the first/second declensions) actually became a *third* declension adjective in the comparative.

First Type	*Comparative Degree*
béllus, -a, -um 'pretty'	béllior, -ius 'prettier'

Second Type	
fórtis, -e 'strong'	fórtior, -ius 'stronger'

The forms *bellior* and *fortior* represent the masculine and feminine nominative singular, while *bellus* and *fortius* represent the corresponding neuter. Needless to say, the comparative degree was declinable in all cases, singular and plural.

b. Classical Latin superlatives, unlike the comparatives, had endings based on the first type of adjective. Thus, adjectives of the third declension became first/second declension superlatives.:

First Type	*Superlative Degree*
béllus, -a, -um 'pretty'	bellíssimus, -a, -um 'prettiest'

Second Type	
fórtis, -e 'strong'	fortíssimus, -a, -um 'strongest'

c. Finally, a few Classical adjectives (those whose stem ended in a vowel) formed the comparative and superlative differently from the ways mentioned above. Instead of adding endings to the adjective, the word *magis* 'more' or *maxime* 'most' preceded it:

idoneus 'suitable'
magis idoneus 'more suitable'
maxime idoneus 'most suitable'

§37. In Vulgar Latin, the comparative and superlative were analytic constructions and not synthetic as in the Classical language. In fact, the system used above (§36c) for adjectives whose stem ended in a vowel was the analytic structure which was adopted by the Romance Languages. Those areas of early Roman conquest, such as Hispania, used *magis* + *adjective*, while those areas of later conquest, such as Gaul, used *plus* + *adjective*. The Vulgar Latin comparatives thus set the basis for Romance:

CL altior > VL magis altus (Sp. más alto)
CL severior > VL magis severus (Sp. más severo)

§38. There were a few Classical Latin comparatives that were totally irregular in form, four of which were retained by Vulgar Latin:

CL meliõrem > VL melióre Sp. mejor)
CL maiõrem > VL maióre (Sp. mayor)
CL peiõrem > VL peióre (Sp. peor)
CL minõrem > VL minóre (Sp. menor)

The Classical Latin superlative in -*íssimus* (§21b) was lost in Vulgar Latin in favor of an analytic construction based on the Vulgar Latin comparative. The reason that Spanish has the suffix -*ísimo* today is that is is learned, taken directly from Classical Latin and restored by scholars during the medieval period.

Latin Pronouns

§39a. Classical Latin had a wealth of demonstrative pronouns. *Hic, haec, hoc*[10] pointed out something near the speaker. To refer to something near the person spoken to, the set *iste, ista, istud* was used. To allude to something already mentioned, *is, ea, id* were used. The pronouns that meant 'the same' were *īdem, eadem, idem*. The intensive pronouns meaning 'oneself' were *ipse, ipsa, ipsum*.

---

[10] The three forms given in this and the following examples represent the masculine, feminine and neuter nominative singular of the pronouns in question. All pronouns were declinable in all cases, singular and plural, and in all three genders.

b. Vulgar Latin did not retain all of the Classical demonstratives. *Hic, haec, hoc* were largely lost, as were *is, ea, id,* most likely due to their lack of phonetic substance. *Iste, ista, istud* replaced the former set (becoming *este, este, esto* in Spanish) and the latter was replaced by *ille, illa, illud* (*él, ella,* and *ello* in modern Spanish). *Īdem, eadem, idem* were lost without leaving a trace while *ipse, ipsa, ipsum* were retained, but without their reflexive value (Sp. *ese, esa, eso*).

§40. The Classical relative pronouns (*quī, quae, quid*) and interrogative pronouns (*quis, quis, quis*) which were almost exactly alike in their declensions, except in the nominative forms, became hopelessly confused in Vulgar Latin, resulting in the fusion of the two into VL *qui, quae, quod.*

The Classical genitive singular of the relative pronouns, *cuius,* which had the same form for all three genders, was continued into Vulgar Latin, but took masculine and feminine endings (as reflected in Sp. *cuyo, cuya*). This is an instance of the retention of a genitive form in Vulgar Latin.

§41. The development of the personal pronouns for the first and second persons from Classical to Vulgar Latin shows some interesting and even surprising features. First, unlike ordinary nouns, personal pronouns retained the dative case as well as the usual nominative and accusative cases:

	Classical Latin	Vulgar Latin	Classical Latin	Vulgar Latin
nom.	ego 'I'	eo	nōs 'we'	nos
dat.	mihi 'to me'	mi	nōbis 'to us'	nos
acc.	mē 'me'	me	nōs us	nos
nom.	tū 'you' *sing.*	tu	vōs 'you' *pl.*	vos
dat.	tibi 'to you'	ti	vōbis 'to you'	vos
acc.	tē you'	te	vōs 'you'	vos

There was a collateral, more emphatic form in Vulgar Latin for the nominative *nos* and *vos: nos alteros* and *vos alteros.* (Modern Spanish *nosotros* and *vosotros*)

The form *ti* is not a direct continuation of *tibi,* but is analogical with *mi.*

The dative *nos* and *vos* are attested in the *Appendix Probi:*

nobiscum non noscum 'with us'
vobiscum non voscum 'with you'

(The preposition *cum* 'with' usually followed Classical pronouns.)

b. The amazing thing about these pronouns in the Vulgar Latin of Hispania was a revolutionary change in function that *mi, me* and *ti, te* underwent. The continuations of datives *mi* and *ti* were no longer used exclusively as datives, but became instead *stressed* pronouns for either dative *or* accusative use (as in Spanish *me lo dio a mí* [*mí* = stressed dative], *me vio a mí* [*mí* = stressed accusative]). The continuations of the accusatives *me* and *te* were no longer used exclusively as accusatives, but became instead *unstressed* datives *or* accusatives (Sp. *te lo dieron* [*te* = unstressed dative], *te vieron* [*te* = unstressed accusative]).

§42. Classical Latin had no personal pronouns *per se* for the third person, but used the *is, ea, id* set of demonstratives when personal pronouns were called for. In Vulgar Latin, the *ille, illa, illum* set replaced *is, ea, id* (§39a):

Singular

		Classical Latin	Vulgar Latin	Spanish
nom.	*m*	ílle 'he'	ílle	él
	f	ílla 'she'	ílla	ella
dat.	*m + f*	illī 'to him/her'	illí	le
acc.	*m*	íllum 'him'	illú	lo
	f	íllam 'her'	illá	la

Plural

nom.	*m*	illī 'they' *m*	íllos	ellos
	f	íllae 'they' *f*	íllas	ellas
dat.	*m + f*	illīs 'to them'	illís	les
acc.	*m*	illōs 'them' *m*	illós	los
	f	illās 'them' *f*	illás	las

It should be noted that the Vulgar Latin nominative forms *illos* and *illas* were analogical, based on the accusative forms, and did not develop from the Classical nominatives. The shift in stress in certain Vulgar Latin forms should also be noticed, for the Vulgar Latin stress was continued into Spanish.

§43. Finally, some mention should be made of the reflexive pronouns. Since this type of pronoun "reflected" the subject, it had no nominative form. The dative and accusative, given below, were the most common cases:

	Classical Latin	Vulgar Latin	Spanish
dat.	mihi 'to myself'	mi	mí
acc.	mē 'myself'	me	me
dat.	tibi 'to yourself'	ti	ti
acc.	tē 'yourself'	te	te
dat.	sibi 'to himself'	si	sí
acc.	sē 'himself'	se	se
dat.	nōbis 'to ourselves'	nos	nos
acc.	nōs 'ourselves'	nos	nos
dat.	vōbis 'to yourself'	vos	os
acc.	vōs 'yourself'	vos	os

Since these forms in most cases are identical with the first and second person pronouns (§41), they evolved in much the same way. For example, *si* is analogical with *mi* and does not continue *sibi*.

§44. The Classical Latin possessives were declined like the first type of adjective (*meus, -a, -um* 'my', for instance). In Vulgar Latin, only the accusative case of the masculine and feminine remained, all other cases having fallen. Examples below are taken from the singular, although there was a plural form as well.

Classical Latin	Vulgar Latin
meum, meam 'my'	meu, mia (§7b)
tuum, tuam 'your'	tuu, tua
suum, suam 'his/her'	suu, sua
nostrum, -am 'our'	nostru, -a
vestrum, -am 'your'	vostru, -a

VL *vostru* is analogical with *nostru*.

§45a. Most numbers through 100 were not declinable in Classical Latin; that is, they had the same form for masculine feminine and neuter genders. 'One', 'two' and 'three', however, were declinable. 'One', *ūnus, -a, -um*, was declinable in the singular only, of course. 'Two' was *duo, -ae, -o*, declined with some irregular forms (including the masculine and neuter [*-ae, -o*] shown in the model).

'Three' was *trēs, trēs, tria,* declined like the plural of the third declension. The result in Vulgar Latin was that only '1' and '2' showed gender distinction, since the neuter was to fall. Examples are shown in the accusative because that was the case that survived:

Classical Latin	Vulgar Latin
ūnus, -am, -um '1'	unu, una
duos, duas, duo '2'	duos, duas
trēs, trēs, tria '3'	tres, tres

From four to ten the numbers showed little differences:

Classical Latin	Vulgar Latin
quattuor '4'	quattor
quīnque '5'	cinque (§13b)
sex '6'	sex
septem '7'	septe
octō '8'	octo
novem '9'	nove
decem '10'	dece

VL *quattor* showed a loss of the second CL *u*; loss of *u* before another vowel was a comon feature of Vulgar Latin.

b. The Vulgar Latin of the Iberian Peninsula made some important changes in the numbers 11 through 19. Although it retained the Classical formation of 11-15, it rejected the Classical Latin formula for 16 through 19 and provided its own solution:

Classical Latin	Vulgar Latin
ūndecim '11'	undece
duodecim '12'	duodece
tredecim '13'	tredece
quattuordecim '14'	quattordece
quīndecim '15'	quindece
sēdecim '16'	dece et sex
septendecim '17'	dece et sette
duodēvīgintī '18'	dece et octo
ūndēvīgintī '19'	dece et nove

c. A major change seen in the development of the tens is the normal loss of -g- (§11b):

Classical Latin	*Vulgar Latin*
vīgintī '20'	viinti
trīginta '30'	triinta
quadrāginta '40'	quadraenta
quīnquāginta '50'	cinquaenta
sexāginta '60'	sexaenta
septuāginta '70'	settaenta
octōginta '80'	octoenta
nōnāginta '90'	novaenta

VL *cinquaenta* is analogical with *cinque* '5' and *novaenta* is analogical with *nove* '9'.

d. 'One hundred' was *centum*, which was undeclinable. Multiples of 100 were declinable like the plural of the first type of adjective: *ducentī, -ae, -a*, for example, *Mille* '1000' was equally not declinable in the "singular", but in multiples it was declined like neuter 'i-stem' third declension nouns (§21b): *duo milia* '2000', for example.

It must be said that most Vulgar Latin numbers cited above have never been attested since numbers were overwhelmingly written as *numerals*, not as words.

The Latin Conjugation Systems

§46. The number of inflected forms of the Classical Latin noun was exceeded only by the number of forms of the Classical Latin verb. Whereas the typical noun had twelve inflected forms, the typical verb had more than 125 forms. The endings of verbs gave even more information than the endings of nouns; they indicated whether the subject was first, second, or third person, singular or plural, identified the TENSE and the MODE, and distinguished whether the verb was ACTIVE or PASSIVE.

a. There were four conjugation groups in Classical Latin, easily identifiable by the ending of the present active infinitive. The first conjugation ended in *-āre* (*amāre* 'to love', *laudāre* 'to praise'), the second ending in *-ēre* (*vidēre* 'to see', *habēre* 'to have'), the third in *-ĕre* (*pōnĕre* 'to put', *fúgĕre* 'to flee'), and the fourth in *-īre* (*venīre* 'to come', *audīre* 'to hear').

The third conjugation was composed of two different subgroups: those with the first person singular present indicative ending in *-ō* (*pōnō* 'I put', and those ending in *-iō* (*fugiō* 'I flee'). This second type retained the *-i-* in certain tenses.

Of the four Classical conjugations, only three survived in the Vulgar Latin of Hispania, details of which will be given later (§51a).

b. Any Classical Latin verb that was ACTIVE (*vídeō* 'I see', *laudō* 'I praise') could be made PASSIVE by substituting a passive ending (*vídeor* 'I am seen', *láudor* 'I am praised'). A complication existed in connection with the active and passive conjugations; there was a type of verb (known as DEPONENT) that was passive in form (i.e., with passive verb endings) but active in meaning: *fábulor*, with its passive ending, meant 'I speak', and *séquor*, equally passive in form, meant 'I follow'.

In Vulgar Latin the entire Classical passive fell and a new one was formed (§61). All Classical deponents either were lost or were rebuilt on an active model (§62).

§47a. Classical Latin had six indicative active tenses. Examples will be given of *audīre* 'to hear'. There were the PRESENT (*audiō* 'I hear'), the PERFECT (*audīvī* 'I heard'), the IMPERFECT (*audiēbam* 'I was hearing), the PLUPERFECT (*audīveram* 'I had heard'), the FUTURE (*audiam* 'I shall hear'), and the FUTURE PERFECT (*audīverō* 'I shall have heard'). Vulgar Latin dropped both Classical future tenses and devised new ways to express them.

There were four subjunctive active tenses. The present (*audiam* 'that I may hear'), the perfect (*audīverim*, used after a present or future verb to mean 'that I might hear'), the imperfect (*audīrem*, used after a past tense verb to mean 'that I might hear'), and the pluperfect (*audīvissem* 'that I might have heard'). Vulgar Latin dropped both the perfect and imperfect subjunctive tenses, replacing them both with the Classical *pluperfect* subjunctive forms, and it created a new pluperfect subjunctive of its own.

The imperative should be mentioned at this point; it had forms only for the second person singular and plural (*audī, audīte* 'hear!') Vulgar Latin retained these, but had to deal with the formation of a negative imperative.

The indicative passive shared the same six tenses with the active: the present (*audior* 'I am heard), the perfect (*audītus sum* 'I was heard'), the imperfect (*audiēbar* 'I was being heard'), the pluperfect (*audītus eram* 'I had been heard'), the future (*audiar* 'I shall be heard'), and the future perfect (*audītus erō* 'I shall have been heard').

The subjunctive passive had the four tenses of the indicative as well: the present (*audiar* 'that I might be heard'), the imperfect (*audīrer* 'that I might be heard), the perfect (*audītus sim* 'that I might be heard'), and the pluperfect (*audītus essem* 'that I might have been heard'). All Classical passives, both indicative and subjunctive, disappeared virtually without leaving a trace and Vulgar Latin remade its own passives.

Classical Latin had four participles. The active participles were the present (*audiēns* 'hearing'), and the future (*audītūrus* 'about to hear'). The passive participles were the perfect (*audītum* '[having been] heard') and the future (*audiendus* 'about to be heard'). Both active participles fell in Vulgar Latin.

There were six different types of infinitives in Classical Latin: the present active (*audīre* 'to hear'), the perfect active (*audīvisse* 'to have heard'), the future active (*audītūrus esse* 'to be about to hear'), the present passive (*audīrī* 'to be heard'), the perfect passive (*audītus esse* 'to have been heard'), and the future passive (*audītum īrī* 'to be going to be heard'). Of the six Classical infinitives, only the present active remained in Vulgar Latin.

Each tense had only six persons: three in the singular (corresponding to 'I', 'you', singular, and 'he/she') and three in the plural (corresponding to 'we', 'you' plural, and 'they'). Classical and Vulgar Latin were like modern English in that there was no distinction made between a familiar and formal 'you'; there was just *tū* for the singular and *vōs* for the plural.

§48. Before the details of the conjugations themselves are given, it must be stated that Classical Latin verbs are traditionally identified by four PRINCIPAL PARTS. A number of tenses, participles, or infinitives build on the stem of each principal part. The first principal part is the first person singular of the present indicative active (*audiō*, for example), the second principal part is the present active infinitive (*audīre*), the third principal part is the first person singular of the perfect indicative active (*audīvī*), and the fourth principal part is the perfect passive participle, which is usually listed in the neuter nominative singular form (*audītum*). It is important for students of Classical Latin to learn all the principal parts since most verbs are not as consistent in their stems as is *audīre* (*audiō, audīre, audīvī, audītum*); here are examples of verbs with divergent principal parts: *cádō, cádĕre, cécidī, cásum* 'fall'; *dīcō, dīcĕre, dīxī, díctum* 'say'; *fáciō, fácĕre, fḗcī, fáctum* 'do', and lastly the verb with the most unrelated of principal parts, *férō, férre, túlī, lā́tum* 'bear'. Vulgar Latin usually maintained a continuation of the four Classical principal parts.

§49. Finally, Classical Latin had a type of verb known as INCHOATIVE or INCEPTIVE. Any given verb usually referred to an action in progress, but an inchoative verb referred to the *beginning* of the action: *hortus flōret* 'the garden is blooming', but *hortus flōrēscet* (the inchoative version) 'the garden begins to bloom'; *tremō* 'I tremble', *tremēsco* 'I begin to tremble'.

All inchoative verbs belonged to the third conjugation, no matter to which conjugation the basic verbs belonged. Infinitives of the first conjugation became *-ắscĕre*, of the second and third became *-ếscĕre*, and of the fourth became *-íscĕre* inchoatives:

I amắre 'to love' > III amắscĕre 'to begin to love'
II flōrḗre 'to bloom' > III flōrḗscĕre 'to begin to bloom'
III trémĕre 'to tremble' > III tremḗscĕre 'to begin to tremble'
IV dormíre 'to sleep' > III dormíscĕre 'to begin to sleep'

The inchoative system was retained in Vulgar Latin but the notion of the beginning of an action inherent in Classical inchoatives was lost. One grammarian, trying to show his readers how they were misusing inchoative verbs, tried to explain: "*Calesco* is not 'I am warm', but rather 'I begin to get warm'." ("*Calesco* non est *caleo*, sed *calere incipio*." Cited by Väänänen, p. 146.) Vulgar Latin even gained new "inchoatives" based on Classical verbs which were not inchoative in meaning: CL *parēre* became VL *parescere* (Sp. parecer), CL *oboedīre* became VL *obedescere* in Hispania (Sp. obedecer), CL *merēre* became VL *merescere* (Sp. merecer).

§50. The development of the Classical Latin present active into Vulgar Latin shows tremendous changes, especially in the third conjugation; complete Classical Latin conjugations are given here so that their development can be easily followed:

	I *laudắre*	II *vidḗre*	III *pónĕre*	III -iō *fúgĕre*	IV *audíre*
ego	láudō	vídeō	pónō	fúgiō	áudiō
tū	láudās	vídēs	pónis	fúgis	áudīs
(is)	láudat	vídet	pónit	fúgit	áudit
nōs	laudắmus	vidḗmus	pónimus	fúgimus	audímus
vōs	laudắtis	vidḗtis	pónitis	fúgitis	audítis
(eī)	láudant	vídent	pónunt	fúgiunt	áudiunt

In the third conjugation, some first person singulars ended in *-o* and others in *-io*—this latter group became known as '*-iō* verbs'.

§51a. In the Iberian Peninsula, the four conjugation groups of Classical Latin were reduced to three through the loss of the Classical third conjugation (*-ĕre*). The members of the Classical third conjugation usually moved to the second conjugation in Vulgar Latin, as shown below. Notice the shift in stress in Vulgar Latin:

> CL cápĕre > VL capére (Sp. caber)
> CL comprehéndĕre > VL comprendére (Sp. comprender)
> CL fácĕre > VL facére (Sp. hacer)
> CL légĕre > VL legére (Sp. leer)
> CL pónĕre > VL ponére (So. poner)
> CL sápĕre > VL sapére (Sp. saber)
> CL véndĕre > VL vendére (Sp. vender)

b. Some Classical Latin third conjugation *-iō-* verbs moved to the Vulgar Latin *-ire* conjugation. This type of third conjugation verb was very much like the Classical fourth conjugation (*-īre*) in most tenses, and exactly alike in the present active (except for vowel length), so the change seemed very natural:

> CL concípĕre (concípiō) > VL concipíre (Sp. concebir)
> CL fúgĕre (fúgiō) > VL fugíre (Sp. huir)
> CL párĕre (páriō) > VL paríre (Sp. parir)
> CL recípĕre (recípiō) > VL recipíre (recibir)
> CL succŭ́tĕre (succŭ́tiō) > VL succutíre (Sp. sacudir)

Not all *-iō* verbs made this shift, however. *Cápĕre* (*cápiō*), *fácĕre* (*fáciō*) (§51a) and *sápĕre* (*sápiō*) went to the Vulgar Latin *-ére* conjugation: *capére, facére, sapére.*

c. A few Classical *second* conjugation verbs also changed to the Vulgar Latin *-ire* conjugation. Since their *-eō* first person singular ending became *-iō* through normal phonetic development in Vulgar Latin, these verbs were swept into the *-ire* group along with the third conjugation *-io* verbs:

> CL implḗre (ímpleō = VL -io) > VL implíre (Sp. henchir)
> CL lūcḗre (lŭ́ceō = VL -io) > VL lucíre (Sp. lucir)
> CL ridḗre (rídeō = VL -io) > VL ridíre (Sp. reír)

§52. The Vulgar Latin indicative shows a number of changes. The minority of Classical Latin verbs which ended in *-io* in the first person singular (some third conjugation verbs and all fourth conjugation verbs), usually lost the yod by analogy with those verbs which had no yod (*laudō, vendō*, etc.), such as CL *faciō* > VL *faco* >

Sp. *hago*. This change also affected the subjunctive (VL *faca* for the CL *faciam*).

The first and second person plural forms of the Classical third conjugation were stressed on the stem, unlike the other conjugation groups (*véndimus, vénditis*, but *laudámus, laudátis*). As the Classical Latin third conjugation fell, the stress moved to the endings in *vendémus, vendétis* to be in line with stress patterns elsewhere.

The third person plural endings in *-unt* ternded to give way to *-ent*. The *Peregrinatio* shows examples such as *absolvent* (for the Classical *absolvunt*), *accipient* (for *accipiunt*), and *exient* (for *exiunt*). Spanish forms had to derive from the endings with *e: legent* gives Sp. *leen*, but *legunt* could have only given the form *léon* which never existed.

§53. The Classical Latin imperative was easy to form, but existed only in the positive. The singular was made by removing the *-s* from the second person singular of the present indicative active, and the plural merely by adding *-te* to the singular command:

láudā 'praise!'	vídē 'see!'	áudī 'hear!'
laudáte	vidéte	audíte

The positive imperative transferred to Vulgar Latin intact.

In Classical Latin, to express a negative imperative, people had to talk around the idea by using the imperative of *nólō* 'be unwilling' and the infinitive of the verb in question:

Nólī laudare! 'Be unwilling to praise! = 'Do not praise!'
Nólīte vidēre! 'Be unwilling to see! = Do not see!'

Nólō was not continued into Vulgar Latin. The negative imperative was borrowed from the negative subjunctive (§§65, 66).

§54. The Classical Latin future was a tense destined to be phonetically unstable and in Vulgar Latin it disappeared virtually without leaving a trace,[11] as the explanation following these examples will show:

I	II	III	IV
laudáre	*vidēre*	*ponēre*	*audíre*
'praise'	'see'	'put'	'hear'
laudábō	vidébō	pónam	áudiam
laudábis	vidébis	pónēs	áudiēs

[11] The second person singular of the future of *esse* 'to be' was *eris*; this form is supposed to have given the Spanish *eres*. If this is true, as it

laudábit	vidébit	pónet	áudiet
laudábimus	vidébimus	pōnḗmus	audiḗmus
laudábitis	vidébitis	pōnḗtis	audiḗtis
laudábunt	vidébunt	pónent	áudient

a. The first conjugation third person singular (*laudābit*) came to be pronounced the same way as the same person of the perfect indicative (*laudāvit*) (§12). The future of the first and second conjugations, with their characteristic -*b*-, resembled their corresponding imperfect systems (*laudābam, vidēbam*). The first person singular of the future in the third and fourth conjugations was exactly like the present subjunctive forms (future *dīcam*, pres. subj. *dīcam;* future *audiam*, pres. subj. *audiam*). Normal phonetic development would cause the forms of the third conjugation future to sound like the corresponding present forms; CL future *dīcēs, dīcēt* would come to sound like VL *dices* (= CL *dīcĭs*), VL *dicet* (= CL *dīcĭt*) of the present tense. Finally, there was no unity of conjugation in the Classical future; that is, while the first and second conjugations presented one type of formation (*laudābō, vidēbō*), the third and fourth conjugations presented another (*pōnam, audiam*).

b. With Vulgar Latin's tendency to be analytic rather than synthetic, the language found an analytic construction already in use with which it could replace the ambiguous Classical future. The construction was of the type *"scrībere habeō"* 'I have to write', *"facere habet"* 'he has to make'. Since anything one has to do *must* be done in the future, the semantic transfer was relatively simple, and the new analytic future became universal in the Western Romance Languages.

It might be mentioned that the Vulgar Latin conjugation of *habere* 'to have' showed shorter forms than its Classical model, possibly because of analogy with other common short verbs (*das, dat,* from *dare* 'to give', *stās, stat* from *stāre* 'to stand') as well as from its new use as an unstressed auxiliary:

áio (CL hábeō)	(ab)émus (CL habḗmus)
as (CL hábes)	abétis (CL habētis)
at (CL hábet)	ant (CL hábent)

Here is an example of this type of future from the Latin Vulgate Bible (see footnote 2 above), which shows Classical spelling for the auxiliary:

---

appears to be, *eres* is the only vestige in Spanish of the ancient future tense.

"Tempestas . . . tollere habet"
'The storm will take away . . ." John 4: 1, 2

There is one early example that shows the fusion of the two forms as in the modern Romance Languages:

"Iustinius dicebat: 'Daras.' " [= dare + as]
'Justinian said: "You will give." '
Fredegarii Chronica, 85, 27.

§55. The fortunate construction with *habere* + *infinitive* was also able to give rise to a conditional tense (which was unknown in Classical Latin). In this case, the imperfect of *habere* was used following an infinitive:

"Sanare te habebat Deus." 'God would cure you.'
Ps.-Aug. *Serm.* 253, 4

§56. The imperfect (or perfect) of *habere*, with the past participle (= Classical passive perfect participle), was used as an alternate analogical pluperfect: CL *posuĕrant* = VL *posita habebant* = Sp. *habían puesto*. This Vulgar Latin example comes from the *Peregrinatio*.

§57a. In Classical Latin, the imperfect indicative conjugations were characterized by *-ba-* in the endings:

I	II	IV
laudábam	vidébam	audiébam
laudábas	vidébas	audiébas
laudábat	vidébat	audiébat
laudābámus	vidēbámus	audiēbámus
laudābátis	vidēbátis	audiēbátis
laudábant	vidébant	audiébant

The normal *-ĕre* verbs shared second conjugation imperfect endings (*pōnébam*), but the *-iō* type shared fourth conjugation endings (*fugiébam*). The shift in stress in the first and second person plural forms above should be noticed.

b. The Vulgar Latin imperfect indicative showed a few notable differences. The first conjugation, with its *-āba-* endings, remained intact; the other conjugations, however, began to lose the *b*, probably becaus of a dissimilation (§149c) of the two *b*'s in the common verbs CL *habēbam* and CL *debēbam* to VL *habea* and *debea*; this

dissimilated ending then spread to all other verbs of the Vulgar Latin -ere and
-*ire* conjugations. Once this happened, the -*éa* changed to -*ía*
according to §7b.

The fourth conjugation -*iēbam* lost its -*i*- in Vulgar Latin by
analogy with the numerous verbs in -*ēbam*; one sees examples of
this loss of -*i*- in inscriptions: VL *audeba* (for CL *audiēbam*), *refuge-
bat* (for CL *refugiēbat*), and *custodebat* (for *custodiēbat*).

Whereas the stress moved forward one syllable in the Classical
Latin first and second person plural of the imperfect (*laudắbam* but
laudābắmus), in the Vulgar Latin of Hispania the stress leveled out
over the same vowel throughout the conjugation (*laudába, laud-
ábas, laudábat, laudábamus, laudábatis, laudábant*).

The irregular imperfects *eram* (of *esse* 'to be') and *ībam* (of *īre*
'to go') were maintained in Vulgar Latin.

§58. In Classical Latin, the perfect tense was used for two different meanings. The first one was that of the perfect proper: 'I
have seen, I have said'. The second was the meaning of what Classical grammarians call the AORIST, or 'simple past' (in Spanish, the
preterite, 'I saw, I said').

In Vulgar Latin, however, the perfect came to be used only in
the meaning of the aorist, the simple past ('I invited', for example).
To fill the semantic gap, Vulgar Latin used the present tense of
habere + past participle. Thus, we see in Gregory of Tours (ca. 538-
ca. 594):

"Episcopam invitatum habes." 'You have invited the bishop.'

The perfect was the most complicated of the tenses, for it was
composed of three different groups: WEAK, STRONG and REDUP-
LICATED.

Weak and strong are not descriptive terms in English, for they
have nothing whatsoever to do with strength *per se*. A weak perfect is merely one that is stressed, in all forms, on the ending
rather than on then stem (*laud-ắvī, aud-ívī*); these verbs are further
characterized by a *v* in their endings. A strong perfect, on the
other hand, is one that is stressed (in three of the six forms) on
the stem rather than the ending (*víd-ī* 'I saw', *háb-uī* 'I had', *pós-uī* 'I
put', *vénī* 'I came').[12] A reduplicated perfect is one in which the first

---

[12] *Weak* and *strong* are translated directly from German. In that language when the stem of a verb can stand alone without an ending, it is
considered 'strong' (*Ich kam*), but if it requires an ending to complete its
meaning, it is considered 'weak' (i.e., unable to stand alone).

syllable of the verb appears twice (usually with a change in vowel): *cádō* 'I fall', *cécidī* 'I fell'.

a. Most of the weak perfects in Classical Latin were of the first and fourth conjugations:

I	IV
laudā́vī	audī́vī
laudāvístī	audīvístī
laudā́vit	audī́vit
laudā́vimus	audī́vimus
laudāvístis	audīvístis
laudāvḗrunt	audīvḗrunt

There were no third conjugation weak perfects since the third conjugation was 'strong' by nature; witness the infinitives: *pónĕre*, *fúgĕre*) The few second conjugation weak perfects had the infinitive vowel *-ē-* before the *v* (*delḗre* 'to destroy', *delḗvī* 'I destroyed'; *implḗre* 'to fill', *implḗvī* 'I filled').

Vulgar Latin weak perfects show a number of important changes. Those of the first and fourth conjugations were continued into Vulgar Latin, but their endings were modified. The first conjugation in Vulgar Latin shows that the *-v-* and the *-i-* (or *-e-*) that follows were lost in the endings of most persons, but only the *-v-* was lost in the first person singular and only the *-i-* was lost in the third singular.

laudā́vī > laudái
laudā(ví)stī > laudásti
laudā́v(i)t > laudáut
laudā́(vi)mus > laudámus
laudā(ví)stis > laudástis
laudā(vḗ)runt > laudárunt

The first conjugation third person singular ending, with its *-v-* having become *-u-* (*áv[i]t > áut*) has been attested in Pompeii.

The fourth conjugation showed the same changes as above in the singular, but had a double development in the plural: either only the *-v-* was lost, or both the *-v-* and the *-i-* (or *-e-*) following it disappeared:

audī́(v)ī > audíi

audī(ví)stī > audísti

audī́v(i)t > audíut

audī́(v)imus > audiémus
audī́(vi)mus > audímus

audī(v)ístis > audiéstis
audī(ví)stis > audístis

audī(v)ḗrunt > audiérunt
audī(vḗ)runt > audírunt

The fourth conjugation already showed alternate endings for the
first person singular in Classical Latin: *-īvī* and *īī*. This latter form
provided an analogical basis for CL *-āvī* to become VL *-ai*.

b. Strong perfects were divided into three groups. First, there
were those with *u* between the stem of the verb and the usual
endings. This type was characteristic of the second conjugation,
although there were a few *u* perfects in the third and fourth conjugations as well (*sápĕre* 'to taste', *sápuī* 'I tasted'; *aperíre* 'to open',
apéruī 'I opened').

habḗre	*tenḗre*	*timḗre*
'to have'	'to hold'	'to fear'
hábuī	ténuī	tímuī
habuístī	tenuístī	timuístī
hábuit	ténuit	tímuit
habúimus	tenúimus	timúimus
habuístis	tenuístis	timuístis
habuḗrunt	tenuḗrunt	timuḗrunt

In Vulgar Latin, this type of perfect either was retained, in
which case the *-u-* changed position with the preceding consonant
(CL *sápuī* > VL *sáupi* > OSp. *sope*, CL *hábuī* > VL *háubi* > OSp.
ove), or the perfect became weak in Vulgar Latin and thus also in
Spanish (CL *tímuī* > VL *timíi* > Sp. *temí*, CL *apéruī* > VL apérii >
Sp. *abrí*).

c. The second group of strong perfects is called SIGMATIC. The
word 'sigmatic' derives from the Greek letter Σ 'sigma' (= s). In this
type of perfect an *s* (or an *x*) is inserted before the ending. The
sigmatic perfect is characteristic of the third conjugation, but a few
second conjugation verbs also have sigmatic perfects (*manḗre* 'to
remain', *mansī* 'I remained').

míttĕre	*scríbēre*	*dícĕre*
'to send'	'to write'	'to say'
mísī	scrípsī	díxī
mīsístī	scrīpsístī	dīxístī
mīsit	scrípsit	díxit
mísimus	scrípsimus	díximus
mīsístis	scrīpsístis	dīxístis
mīsḗrunt	scrīpsḗrunt	dīxḗrunt

The sigmatic perfects remained in Vulgar Latin and a few new ones were even created there, notably CL *quaesívī* > VL *quési* > Sp. *quise*. The change from weak to strong in the preceding example is often hard for the novice to see; in the Classical example, the stress comes on the ending ‖[after the *s*] (therefore it is weak); while in the Vulgar Latin example, the stress is on the stem [preceding the *s*] (therefore it is strong).

d. The third group of strong perfects had nothing inserted between the stem and the ending, but the vowel of the stem was usually lengthened or raised to a higher point of articulation. This type of perfect was almost evenly divided between the second and third conjugations, although there were a few fourth conjugation perfects of this type, notably *veníre* 'to come', *vḗnī* 'I came'.

fắcĕre	*vĭdḗre*	*lĕ́gĕre*
'to make'	'to see'	'to read'
(ă > ē)	(ĭ > ī)	(ĕ > ē)
fḗcī	vídī	lḗgī
fēcístī	vīdístī	lēgístī
fḗcit	vídit	lḗgit
fḗcimus	vídimus	lḗgimus
fēcístis	vīdístis	lēgístis
fēcḗrunt	vīdḗrunt	lēgḗrunt

This group was maintained virtually intact in Vulgar Latin: CL *féci* > VL *féci*, CL *vídī* > VL *vídi*, CL *lḗgī* > VL *légi*, CL *vḗnī* > VL *véni*.

e. Finally, there were the REDUPLICATED perfects. This type of perfect was the norm in Ancient Greek, but there were not many in Classical Latin. Most of these were of the third conjugation, but *two* first conjugation verbs, *dáre* 'to give' (conjugated below) and *stáre* 'to stand', *stḗtī* 'I stood', also had reduplicated perfects. This type of perfect showed great vowel alternation:

cádere	*cúrrere*	*dáre*
'to fall'	'to run'	'to give'
cécidī	cucúrrī	dédī
cecidístī	cucurrístī	dedístī
cécidit	cucúrrit	dédit
cecídimus	cucúrrimus	dédimus
cecidístis	cucurrístis	dedístis
cecidērunt	cucurrērunt	dedērunt

All perfects of this type, with the exception of *dédī* (from *dáre*) and *stḗtī* (from *stáre*) were rebuilt to fit regular weak patterns: CL *cucúrrī* was rebuilt as VL *curríi* and gave Sp. *corrí*; CL *cécidī* was rebuilt as VL *cadíi* and gave Sp. *caí*.

§59. The Classical perfect passive participle, like the perfect tense, could be weak or strong, and with the same distribution: the first and fourth conjugations usually had weak perfect passive participles, and the second and third conjugations had strong ones for the most part.

a. The perfect participle of the first and fourth conjugations had a stem like that of the infinitive. To the stem was added -*ātum* for the first conjugation and -*ītum* for the fourth (*laudātum* 'praised', *audītum* 'heard'). Participles were fully declinable, using the system of the first type of adjective (§35a).

The few second conjugation verbs which had a weak passive participle merely added -*ētum* to the stem: *dēlḗre* 'to destroy', *dēlḗtum* 'destroyed', *implḗre* 'to fill', *implḗtum* 'filled'.

The small number of third conjugation weak particples added the ending -*ūtum* to the stem: *consúěre* 'to sew', *consútum* 'sewn'; *battúěre* 'to fight', *battútum* 'fought'.

b. Strong perfect participles usually had a different stem from either the infinitive or the perfect, and there was usually no vowel (-*ā*-, -*ē*-, -*ū*, -*ī*-) bewteen the stem and the ending:

> cápěre 'to take', cáptum 'taken'
> cláuděre 'to close', cláusum 'closed'
> dícěre 'to say', díctum 'said'
> légěre 'to read', léctum 'read'
> míttěre 'to send', míssum 'sent'
> póněre 'to put', pósitum 'put'
> scríběre 'to write', scríptum 'written'
> víncěre 'to conquer', víctum 'conquered'

miscēre 'to mix', míxtum 'mixed'
vidēre 'to see', vīsum 'seen'

A few second and third conjugation verbs, however, did have 'regular' strong perfect participles ending in -ĭtum (but here the i was short and not long): habēre 'to have', hábitum 'had'; bíbĕre 'to drink', bíbitum 'drunk'; trádĕre 'to surrender', tráditum 'surrendered'.

One fourth conjugation verb was also strong in the perfect participle: venīre 'to come', véntum > 'come'.

§60. Vulgar Latin favored the weak participles over the strong; many strong Classical participles were replaced in Vulgar Latin by weak ones: CL sénsum > VL sentítu > Sp. sentido; CL sáltum > VL salítu > Sp. salido; CL véntum > VL venítu > Sp. venido. A number of strong past participles, however, were carried into Vulgar Latin: VL fáctu (Sp. hecho), VL díctu (Sp. dicho), VL pósitu (Sp. puesto), VL scríptu (Sp. escrito), VL mórtu [CL mórtuum] (Sp. muerto), VL rúptu (Sp. roto), VL vístu [CL vīsum] (Sp. visto).

Among the weak participles, those in -ātum, -ūtum and -ītum regularly remained, but the participles in -ētum (representing the Classical second conjugation) disappeared since the second conjugation verbs with weak participles either fell out of use or changed conjugation groups.

§61a. In Classical Latin, there were two ways that the passive was formed, according to the tense involved. A number of tenses (the present indicative and subjunctive, the imperfect indicative and subjunctive, and the future) had a 'synthetic passive', that is, the ending of the verb told that it was passive:

videō 'I see'
videor 'I am seen'

audiēmus 'we shall hear'
audiēmur 'we shall be heard'

b. The compound, 'analytic' passives used a combination of esse 'to be' with the perfect passive participle. The workings of this tense often seem particularly confusing to the modern learner of Classical Latin because the tense of esse seems out of step with the meaning of the passive tense itself. For example, the perfect passive was built using the present of esse plus the perfect passive participle and the pluperfect passive was built using the imperfect of esse and the perfect participle. These examples illustrate this seeming incongruity:

sum 'I *am*'
audītus sum 'I *was* heard'

erās 'you *were*'
missus erās 'you *had been* sent

When one makes a more literal translation, however, these passives *do* make logical sense: *audītum* is a perfect *passive* participle, thus is to be translated 'in the state of having been heard'. So *audītus sum* means 'I am in the state of having been heard', or, with less verbiage, 'I *was* heard'; *missus erās* = 'You were (in the state of) [having been] sent' = 'You had been sent'.

Vulgar Latin dropped all of the 'synthetic' passives (the *audior* type), and remade the passive based on the Classical 'analytical' (*audītus sum*) formation. In doing so, the past participle came to lose the perfective passive notion it had had in Classical Latin; so *audītus sum*, which had meant 'I was heard' in Classical Latin, came to mean 'I *am* heard' in Vulgar Latin. The Classical construction was just as 'illogical' to Vulgar Latin speakers as it usually is to novice learners of Classical Latin today.

The perfect passive in Vulgar Latin, then, became *laudatus fui* 'I was praised'.

§62. Deponent verbs (§46b), which were conjugated as passives but were active in meaning in Classical Latin, usually became active in form in Vulgar Latin. (The infinitives listed below, with their final long -*i*, are examples of the formation of the Classical present passive infinitive.)

CL fabulor 'I speak'	VL fabulo
fabulārī 'to speak'	fabulare (Sp. hablar)
luctor 'I fight'	lucto
luctārī	luctare (Sp. luchar)
morior 'I die'	morio
morī 'to die'	morire (Sp. morir)
sequor 'I follow'	sequo
sequī 'to follow'	sequire (Sp. sequir)

Those Classical deponents which did not go to the regular conjugations were absorbed into the inchocative system (§49): CL *patior* 'to suffer', *patī* 'I suffer' became VL *patescere* (Sp. padecer).

§63. There were a few Classical verbs that had more than one stem in the *same* tense, and a few verbs that had tenses seemingly not built on *any* of the principal parts (notably the present and imperfect of *esse* 'to be', the present of *velle* 'to desire', and the present and imperfect of *īre* 'to go'). Classical Latin grammarians call these the irregular verbs, and there were only about a half dozen of them.

Four will be given here in a sampling of tenses. Here are their principal parts:

> 'to be' *sum, ésse, fúī,* ——
> 'to be able' *póssum, pósse, pótuī,* ——
> 'to desire' *vólō, vélle, vóluī,* ——
> 'to go' *éō, íre, íī, ítum*

The irregular infinitive (lacking *r*) of the first three should be noted, as well as their lack of the perfect passive participles.

Present Active Indicative

sum	póssum	vólō	éō
es	pótes	vīs	īs
est	pótest	vult	it
súmus	póssumus	vólumus	ímus
éstis	potéstis	vúltis	ítis
sunt	póssunt	vólunt	éunt

Imperfect Active Indicative

éram	póteram	volēbam	íbam
érās	póterās	volēbās	íbam
érat	póterat	volēbat	íbat
erámus	poterámus	volēbámus	ibámus
erátis	poterátis	volēbátis	ibátis
érant	póterant	volēbant	íbant

Perfect Active Indicative

fúī	pótuī	vóluī	íī
fuístī	potuístī	voluístī	ístī
fuít	pótuit	vóluit	íit
fúimus	potúimus	volúimus	íimus
fuístis	potuístis	voluístis	ístis
fuērunt	potuērunt	voluērunt	iērunt

Vulgar Latin did not tolerate as much irregularity as Classical Latin, and it regularized whatever it could: the infinitives were easily rebuilt based on conjugated forms to conform to 'regular' patterns. *Esse* became VL *éssere*; *velle* became VL *volére* (rebuilt on its perfect form *vólui*); and *posse* became *potére* (Sp. poder) also rebuilt on its perfect, *pótui*. The present tense of *potere* was based on its new infinitive: *póteo, pótes, pótet, potémus, potétis, pótent*. Although the conjugation of *ire* already conformed to normal patterns, its conjugated forms were much too short, amounting only to endings and nothing more. The forms of *ire* were substituted in most tenses in Vulgar Latin by those of *vadére* 'to walk'.

Ferre 'to bear', which was the most irregular Latin verb (§48), was lost in Vulgar Latin, as might be expected; it was replaced by *portare* in some areas and by *levare* in the Iberian Peninsula (Sp. llevar). The compounds of *ferre*, however, did manage to remain by changing to the *-ire* conjugation group: CL *sufferre* became VL *sufferire*, CL *offerre* became VL *offerire*, later to take the inchoative suffix and become *ofrecer* in Spanish.

§64. There were other Classical verbs that were lost since they seemingly did not have enough phonetic substance, and they were replaced by longer equivalents in Vulgar Latin. CL *édere* became *comedére* in Hispania (Sp. comer), CL *scire* yielded to VL *sapére* (< CL *sápere*), CL *flére* was lost in favor of *plorare* in Vulgar Latin (Sp. llorar), CL *émere* fell, replaced by VL *comperare* (Sp. comprar).

§65. The present subjunctive effectively was based on the first person singular of the present indicative, without the *-ō* (I *laud-*, II *vide-*, III *pōn-, fugi-*, IV *audi-*). The third conjugation, not given below, had the same endings shared by the second and fourth conjugations:

I	II	IV
láudem	vídeam	áudiam
láudēs	vídeās	áudiās
láudet	vídeat	áudiat
laudḗmus	videámus	audiámus
laudḗtis	videátis	audiátis
láudent	vídeant	áudiant

This tense was basically retained in Vulgar Latin with little change. It was in the remaining tenses that the subjunctive showed important changes in Vulgar Latin. The imperfect subjunctive (CL *laudā-*

rem, audīrem) and the perfect subjunctive, with loss of *-ve-* in the first and fourth conjugations (CL *laudā[ve]rim, audī[ve]rim*) came to have the same pronunciation in Vulgar Latin since the CL *-rem* and *-rim* would both become VL *-re*. As a result, *both* tenses were lost, and the *pluperfect* subjunctive, with a loss of *-vi-* (*laudā[vi]ssem, audī[vi]ssem*), moved up to take over the function of the lost perfect and imperfect subjunctives (Väänänen §307).

§66. To make verbs negative, Classical Latin used one of two words, *nōn* or *nē*, depending on the grammatical context. *Nōn* was used for ordinary, 'indicative' negation:

> Ego Romanus nōn sum. 'I am not a Roman.'
> Ea amīca mea nōn est. 'She is not my friend'

For the type of negation to indicate prohibition, Classical Latin used *nē*:

> Monuit eōs nē hoc facerent. 'He warned them not to do it.'
> Hortor eum nē veniat. 'I exhort him not to come.'

Sometimes, however, the use of *nōn* encroached on the territory of *nē*. A quotation from Terence (185-159 B.C.), in which prohibition is clearly implied, shows this encroachment: "*Non tē credas Davom ludere.*" 'Don't think you're playing Davos.' Petronius (first century A.D.), noted for a style which consciously introduced Vulgar Latin grammar and vocabulary (§1, p. 2), wrote this example in which *nōn* substitutes for *nē*: " . . . *et mē nōn facias ringentem.*" 'and don't make me gnash my teeth.' In the Vulgar Latin of Hispania, however, the complication was resolved when *non* took over both functions.

Other negative words in Classical Latin included *nullus* 'none', *nemo* 'no one', *nihil* 'nothing' and *numquam* 'never'; all of these fell in Hispania except the last.

Classical Latin had no word that meant 'yes'. In an affirmative answer, the style was to repeat the verb of the question in the positive form to mean 'yes', as in modern Portuguese. Here is an example from Plautus (ca. 254-184 B.C.): "*Tuus servus est? Meus est.*" 'Is this your slave? Yes.'

A reinforcing word, such as *certē* 'certainly', *verum* 'true', or *sīc* 'thus', was sometimes used in the response, and many times these words became the whole answer. This example from Terence shows the genesis of the Spanish *sí*: "*Illa maneat? Sīc.*" 'Is she the one who is staying? Yes.'

Adverbs

§67a. Adverbs were formed in two different ways, depending on which type of adjective they were built on. To make an adverb based on the first type of adjective (1st or 2nd declensions), -ē was added to the stem of the adjective:

> mágnus 'great'—mágnē 'greatly'
> líberus 'free'—líberē 'freely'
> Romanicus 'Roman'—románicē 'in a Roman way'

To form an adverb based on the second type of adjective (3rd declension), the ending -*iter* was added to the genitive stem:

Nominative	Genitive
fórtis	fórtis 'strong'—fórtiter 'strongly'
félīx	félīcis 'happy'—félīciter 'happily'
céler	céleris 'swift'—celériter 'swifter'

b. The comparative and superlative of adverbs were formed in this way: -*ius* replaced either -ē or -*iter* to make the comparative, and -*íssimē* replaced the same endings to make the superlative:

líberē	lībérius	líberíssimē
'freely'	*'more freely'*	*'mosty freely'*

fórtiter	fórtius	fortíssimē
'strongly'	*'more strongly'*	*'most strongly'*

There were a few irregular comparative and superlative adverb formations, notably those of *bene* and *male:*

> béne 'well'—mélius 'better'—óptimē 'best'
> mále 'badly'—péius 'worse'—péssimē 'worst'

§68. Vulgar Latin, as a rule, did not continue the usual Classical formation of adverbs by adding -ē or -*iter* to adjectives. There is, however, one curious remnant of the -ē adverb which has survived in Spanish as a noun. *Fabulārī romanicē* 'to speak in the Roman way [i.e., to speak Latin]' became *hablar romance* in Spanish.

Vulgar Latin preferred to form adverbs in this way: *mente*, the ablative of the feminine noun *mens* 'mind', was used following an adjective (which also, naturally, had to be feminine in form). Originally, the two parts were separated: *bona mente* 'with a good mind = well', *devota mente* 'with a devoted mind = devotedly', *intrepida mente* 'with an intrepid mind = intrepidly'. The comparative and superlative of adverbs in Vulgar Latin were formed like the comparative and superlative of adjectives, preceded by *magis* or *plus*.

A number of Classical adverbs (of time, place, etc.) did not derive from adjectives: *étiam* 'even', *íam* 'already', *sīc* 'thus', *támen* 'nevertheless', *sémper* 'always', *únde* 'from which', *quōmodo* 'in what way', *súbitō* 'suddenly', *sémel* 'one time', *pósteā* 'afterwards', *hic* 'here', and others. A few of these (*íam, sīc, semper, unde, quōmodo*) were continued into Spanish.

Prepositions

§69. Many Classical prepositions were never used in popular speech, and therefore disappeared from the language. *Apud* gave way to *ad* (Sp. a), *ex* when by itself yielded to *de* (Sp. de), and *ob* to *pro* (Sp. por). Vulgar Latin sometimes combined two or three prepositions with similar meaning in its quest for emphasis; among these were *de ex post* (Sp. después), *de trans* (Sp. detrás), *de in ante* (Sp. delante).

Latin Syntax

§70. Because Classical Latin words bore their own grammatical identification, word order was not as stringent as in an analytic language such as English. For example, no matter where the word *pater* 'father' appeared in the sentence, it had to be the subject since it was in the nominative case. No matter where the word *filium* 'son' appeared in the sentence, it had to be the direct object since it was in the accusative case. No matter where the word *videt* 'sees' was in the sentence, the noun in the nominative case would always be its subject. Therefore, all of the following were possible, and all mean 'The father sees the son', each with a slight 'shade' of emphasis.

1. Pater filium videt.
2. Pater videt filium.
3. Filium pater videt.
4. Filium videt pater.
5. Videt pater filium.
6. Videt filium pater.

§71. In practice, however, for a normal sentence, the first example (*Pater filium videt*) was the usual pattern: subject, direct object, verb. If there were other elements in a sentence, this was the usual order: 1) subject, 2) indirect object, 3) direct object, 4) adverbial modifiers, 5) verb. For example, *"Cicero amicīs litteras saepe scrīpsit. "* 'Cicero often wrote letters to friends.'

Classical Latin syntax placed the most important element at the end of the sentence as in modern Spanish; in most declarative sentences, the verb was the most important element, and that accounts for its common final position. However, to answer the question *"Quem videt pater?"* 'Whom does the father see?', the most important element in the answer would be the answer word (*filium*), so in this particular case, the second example from above would be the best solution (*Pater videt filium*).

Whereas there were a great number of possible syntactic combinations, all of which *could* be understood, the standard spoken language did not come close to using them all.

Vulgar Latin did not permit the flexible syntax of Classical Latin, but depended, as analytic languages must, on a rather fixed word order. It also showed certain grammatical relationships (again as analytic languages do) largely by prepositions preceding nouns rather than endings following them, as the attested examples in the next sections will show.

§72. The accusative gradually took over the functions of the other oblique cases (§27) by becoming the object of different prepositions. The genitive function was usually seen as *de + accusative:*

    CL gen. mulieris = VL de muliere 'of a woman'
    CL gen. multōrum = VL de multos 'of many'

The dative was assumed by ad + *accusative:*

    CL dat. carnificī = VL *ad carnifice* 'to the executioner'

The ablative was the case most frequently governed by a preposition in Classical Latin, yet the accusative took over even the ablative use:

    CL abl. ab hortō = VL ab hortu 'from the garden'
    CL abl. cum iūmentō = VL cum iumentu 'with the mule'

§73. Since Classical Latin had a word order that was not absolutely rigid, it can be imagined that some device must have been needed to differentiate a declarative sentence from an interrogative one. Such a device did exist.

To make an ordinary declarative sentence into a question, the particle *-ne* was attached to the first word of the sentence:

Venīsne? 'Are you coming!'
Vidistīne meum fratrem? 'Did you see my brother?'

If a positive answer was expected, the word *nonne* began the question:

Nonne venīs? 'You're coming, aren't you?'
Nonne vidistī fratrem meum? 'You saw my brother, didn't you'

If a negative answer was expected, the word *num* started the question:

Num venīs? 'You're not coming, are you?'
Num vidistī fratrem meum? 'You didn't see my brother, did you?'

These question markers fell in Vulgar Latin, and word order (coupled probably with varied intonation) replaced them.

§74a. One of the distinctive constructions in Classical Latin was the INFINITIVE WITH SUBJECT ACCUSATIVE. If the action of a subject and a verb (*ego veniō* 'I come', *tū remanēs* 'you remain') was reported after a verb of saying, thinking, or perceiving, the subject was recorded in the accusative and the verb turned into an infinitive:

Ego veniō. Dīcunt mē venīre.
'I come. They say that I come.'

Tū remanēs. Crēdunt tē remanēre.
'You remain. They believe that you remain.'

If the action happened prior to the time of recording, the perfect infinitive was used:

Ego vēnī. Dicunt mē vēnisse.
'I came. They say that I came.'

Tū remansistī. Crēdunt tē remansisse.
'You remained. They believe that you remained.'

b. This construction had another function, which, in the Romance Languages, would be the subjunctive. It is strikingly similar to its English translation:

Coēgērunt mē īre. 'They forced me to go.'
Coēgimus eōs remanēre. We forced them to remain.'

c. In Vulgar Latin this construction, which was so characteris-

tic of Classical Latin, disappeared completely. The Vulgar Latin
replacement for this lost structure used *quia* or *quod* plus a conjugated verb. These examples are extremely close to their Romance
equivalents:

> Nesciebat quia Jesus erat. 'He did not know that Jesus existed.'
> Credimus quod mentis. 'We believe that you are lying.'

§75a. Another typical construction of Classical Latin involved
the use of the SUPINE. This verb form was based on the perfect
passive participle and had two forms: the first ended in -*um*, and
the second ended in -*ū*. The first form of the supine was used after
a verb of motion to express purpose, and is translated by an
infinitive:

> Veniō lectum. 'I come to read.'
> Eunt victum. 'They go to conquer.'

b. The second form of the supine was used after an adjective
such as *difficilis* 'difficult', *facilis* 'easy', *ūtilis* 'useful', *turpis* 'shame-
ful', and *bonus* 'good', and is again translated in English by an
infinitive:

> facilis dictū 'easy to say'
> bonus visū 'good to see'
> ūtilis factū 'useful to do'

In Vulgar Latin, the supine equally disappeared. The first use of
the supine, *veniō lectum* 'I come to read', began to be replaced even
in Classical Latin by a construction using the future passive participle (§47a), *veniō ad legendum*. This construction laid the foundation
for the Vulgar Latin solution, *venio ad legere* (Sp. vengo a leer).
The second use of the supine, *facilis dictū* 'easy to say', was
replaced by *facile ad dicere* in Vulgar Latin (Sp. fácil a decir).

§76. The Classical Latin subjunctive did not have the same sub-
ordinating conjunctions that the modern Romance Languages use.
It used *ut* 'in order that, so that' and *nē* 'so that . . . not' as its main
conjunctions.

> Imperat nōbis ut veniāmus. 'He comands us to come.'
> Imperat nōbis nē remaneāmus. 'He commands us not to
>   remain.'
> Hoc legimus ut discāmus. 'We read this in order to learn.'
> Hoc dīcunt nē eum offendant. 'They say this so they won't
>   offend him.'

The conjunctions *nē* and *ut* were lost in Vulgar Latin and were replaced by *quod*. For example, CL *imperat nōbis ut veniāmus* would be *imperat nos quod veniamus* in Vulgar Latin. In addition, infinitives replaced some subjunctives:

> CL Vadunt ut orent = VL Vadent orare 'They come to plead.'
> CL Venit aliquis ut audiat = VL Venit aliquis audire 'Some-
> one comes to hear.

Through this summary of features of Classical and Vulgar Latin important to the development of Spanish, the necessary linguistic groundwork has been done. What follows is the description of how the phonology and morphology of Vulgar Latin evolved in the normal, regular way as well as through the irregular, exceptional way, into modern Spanish.

✸ 2 ✸

Sound Change Through Time:

Historical Phonetics

Stressed Vowels

§77. The stressed Vulgar Latin vowels were very strong and very stable. Each of the seven Vulgar Latin stressed vowels has a corresponding vowel in modern Spanish. Vulgar Latin stress overwhelmingly carried through to the modern Spanish word no matter how much phonetic change the word underwent, as the examples below show:

Vulgar Latin	*Spanish*
mátre	mádre
cóllocat	cuélga
artículu	artéjo
rápidu	ráudo
muliére (§7c)	mujér
convénit (§17b)	conviéne
tenébras (§17c)	tiniéblas

§78. The chart below. which follows the outline of the vowel triangle (§3), shows the development of stressed vowels from Classical Latin to Spanish:

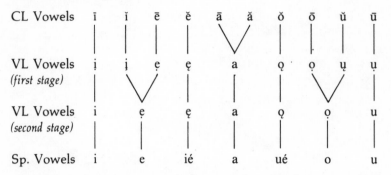

| CL Vowels | ī | ĭ | ē | ĕ | ā | ă | ŏ | ō | ŭ | ū |

VL Vowels (first stage): į i e ę a ǫ o ų u

VL Vowels (second stage): i e ę a ǫ o u

Sp. Vowels: i e ié a ué o u

The complete development from Classical Latin to modern Spanish is given for two reasons: first, in the sections that follow, Classical Latin examples wil be alluded to frequently, and second, Vulgar Latin examples are usually spelled according to the *first stage*, as explained in the footnote to page 6.

It should be noticed that the symmetry of stressed vowel development has continued into Spanish. The two vowels at the extremes of the vowel triangle and the one in the middle have remained pure, but the ones flanking the middle have diphthongized in Spanish. The development of Spanish vowels in initial, final, and pre- or post-tonic positions is also symmetrical, as will be seen.

The sections that follow show in general what happened to the individual stressed vowels. A few special cases and common exceptions are also included, but vowel inflections due to a following yod will be treated in later sections (§104-110).

§79. The Vulgar Latin stressed *i* (from CL *i*) remained without change:

fįcu > higo	lįtigat > lidia
fįlu > hilo	lixįva > lejía
fįliu > hijo	scrįptu > escrito
vįnea > viña	vįte > vid
vįnu > vino	

§80a. The Vulgar Latin stressed *ę* (from CL *ĭ, ē, oe*) generally remained as *e:*

Vulgar Latin examples from CL *ǐ* (usually spelled with *i* in Vulgar Latin transcriptions):

bịbit > bebe	pịlu > pelo
cịlia > ceja	sịnu > seno
cịppu > cepo	strịctu > estrecho
cịrca > cerca	vịr(i)de > verde
lịngua > lengua	vịtta > veta

Vulgar Latin examples from CL *ē:*

cębu > cebo	ręte > red
monęta > moneda	sęta > seda
plęnu > lleno	tęla > tela

Vulgar Latin examples from CL *oe:*

fędu (CL foedum) > feo   pęna (CL poenam) > pena

CL *nịvem* uncharacteristically became *nęve* in the Vulgar Latin of Hispania. This latter form gave rise to the Sp. *nieve*.

  b. In hiatus, the VL *ę* (from CL *ị) rose to i:*

vęa (CL *vǐa*) > vía

§81a. The Vulgar Latin stressed *ę* (from CL *ě, ae*) generally diphthongized to *ié*. The process seems to have been that the Vulgar Latin vowel first lengthened and diphthongized to [eé], then the first element became a yod.

cęntu > ciento	mętu > miedo
cęrtu > cierto	nębula > niebla
cęrvu > ciervo	pęde > pie
ęremu > yermo	pęlle > piel
ęqua > yegua	pęrdo > pierdo
fęsta > fiesta	pętra > piedra

Vulgar Latin examples from CL *ae:*

cęcu (CL *caecum*) > ciego	gręcu(CL *graecum*) > griego
cęlu (CL *caelum*) > cielo	quęro (CL *quaero*) > quiero

Diphthongization took place whether the stressed syllable was OPEN (that is, ending in a vowel: *pé-*de, *né-*bu-la) or CLOSED (that is, ending in a consonant, and therefore closed by it: *pér-*do, *cén-*tu). This feature is unusual since other Romance Languages will diphthongize only in open syllables.

b. In some instances the Vulgar Latin stressed ę first became *ié* in the normal fashion, then was reduced to *i* during the period of Old Spanish.

i. When the Vulgar Latin stressed ę was in haitus, it first diphthongized, thus creating a TRIPHTHONG (i.e., *three* vowel sounds in the same syllable). The triphthong was then simplified by eliminating the middle element:

> meu > mieo > mío
> iudeu > iudieo > judío

ii. The Vulgar Latin endings *-ellu* and *-ella* developed to *-iello* [yɛʎyo] and -iella [yɛʎya] in Old Spanish. Due to the seemingly excessive number of vowel sounds in close proximity, the 'middle' element was again lost, leaving *-illo* [íʎyo] and *-illa* [íʎya]:

> VL castęllu > OSp. castiello > Sp. castillo
> VL cultęllu > OSp. cuchiello > Sp. cuchillo
> VL martęllu > OSp. martiello > Sp. martillo
> VL sęlla > OSp. siella > Sp. silla

Following a consonant cluster known as MUTA CUM LIQUIDA (i.e., a stop or a SPIRANT[1]+ *l* or *r*), diphthongs usually simplified:

> VL intęgro > OSp. en*t*riego > Sp. entrego
> VL pręssa > OSp. *p*riessa > Sp. prisa
> VL pręstu > OSp. *p*riesto > Sp. presto

§82. The stressed VL *a* (from CL ă or ā) remained as *a* in Spanish:

ánnu > año	mátre > madre
cápra > cabra	pátre > padre
cáput > cabo	plátea > plaza
flámma > llama	plánu > llano
mánu > mano	sánguine > sangre

§83a. The Vulgar Latin stressed ǫ (from CL ŏ) diphthongized to *ué*:

---

[1] A spirant (also called a FRICATIVE) is a sound (unvoiced or voiced) where air is released under pressure through a constricted opening. Unvoiced spirants include [s, š, x, f, θ). Voiced spirants include [β, δ, γ, v, z, ȝ].

bǫnu > bueno	mǫrte > muerte
cǫrvu > cuervo	nǫve > nueve
cǫva > cueva	pǫnte > puente
fǫrte > fuerte	pǫrta > puerta
mǫla > muela	sǫrte > suerte

The mechanics of this change are more complicated the change from stressed ę to *ié*. Here, the vowel seems to have lengthened and diphthongized to [oó], then the first element became the back semi-vowel [w], yielding *uó* (the stage in which modern Italian has remained: *buono, nuovo*). Certain Old Spanish dialects also document this stage of development: *puode, tuorto*. The o element then began to move away from the [w] element, following the outline of the vowel triangle (§3) first to *uá* (OSp. *puarta, uamne* [*hombre*]), then to its final form *ué*.

This diphthongization also took place whether the syllable was open or closed.

b. A nasal consonant (i.e., *m* or *n*) sometimes impeded the diphthongization of the stressed ǫ by closing it to ọ.

> cǫmite > conde
> họmine > hombre
> mǫnte > monte

In Old Spanish dialects, the first two of the examples above were seen with diphthongized vowels, but none has survived in modern Castilian (OSp. *cuende, uemne* [= *hombre*]).

However, in many cases the stressed ǫ did diphthongize before a nasal sound:

sǫmnu > sueño	pǫnte > puente
dǫmnu > dueño	frǫnte > OSp. fruente
fǫnte > fuente	

c. The [w] element of the diphthong was sometimes absorbed by the *muta cum liquida* cluster (§81), leaving only the *e*:

> frǫnte > fruente > frente
> flǫccu > flueco > fleco

§84. Classical Latin *au*, which started to become ǫ already in Vulgar Latin, developed to *o* in Spanish:

auca > oca	causa > cosa
auru > oro	fauce > hoz
caule > col	mauru > moro

paucu > poco	tauru > toro
paup(e)re > pobre	thesauru > tesoro

Au first changed to *óu* (the stage which is usually retained in modern Portuguese: *ouro, mouro, pouco, touro*). From here, the diphthong simplified to *o*. The Spanish langauge, therefore, rejected both the *uó* and the *óu* diphthongs (§83a).

§85. The Vulgar Latin stressed ǫ (from CL ō and ŭ), gave *o* in Spanish.

Vulgar Latin examples from CL ŭ (spelled with *u* in inscriptions):

cepu̧lla > cebolla	pu̧teu > pozo
cu̧ppa > copa	pu̧tre > podre
lu̧mbu > lomo	ru̧ptu > roto
mu̧sca > mosca	tu̧rre > torre
pu̧llu > pollo	

Vulgar Latin examples from CL ō:

hǫra > hora	tǫtu > todo
ratiǫne > razón	vǫta > boda

CL *nŭcem* should have given *noz* in Spanish. Sp. *nuez* goes back to a Vulgar Latin form with ǫ: *nǫce*.

§86. The Vulgar Latin stressed u̧ (from CL ū) remained in Spanish:

acu̧tu > agudo	mu̧tu > mudo
du̧ru > duro	scu̧tu > escudo
fu̧mu > humo	su̧cidu > sucio
legu̧m(i)ne > legumbre	tu̧ > tú
mu̧ru > muro	u̧nu > uno

Initial Vowels

§87. An initial vowel is the unstressed vowel found in the first syllable of a word (*ra*-tió-ne, *sus*-péc-ta); it does not necessarily mean that the vowel actually *begins* the word, although such can be and often is the case (*a*-rá-nea, [*h*]*i*-ber-nu).

After the stressed vowels, the initial vowels were the strongest group; only rarely was one lost. The chart below shows the development of initial vowels from Classical Latin to Spanish:

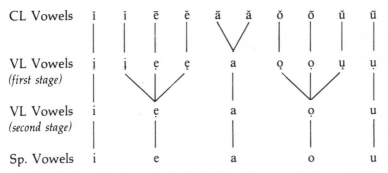

CL Vowels	ī	ĭ	ē	ĕ	ā	ă	ŏ	ō	ŭ	ū
VL Vowels (first stage)	i̧	i̧	ę	ę̧	a	ǫ	o̧	u̧	u̧
VL Vowels (second stage)	i		ę		a		o̧		u
Sp. Vowels	i		e		a		o		u

The evolution of initial vowels from Classical Latin to Spanish is again perfectly symmetrical. It should be noticed that pretonic *e*'s and *o*'s were ultimately close vowels in Vulgar Latin.

§88. The initial VL *i̧* (from CL *ĭ*) remained intact in Spanish:

ci̧vitáte > ciudad	li̧mitáre > lindar
fi̧láre > hilar	ri̧pária > ribera
hi̧bérnu > invierno	ti̧tióne > tizón

Classical Latin *rīdēre* and *dīcēre* developed exceptionally into *reír* and *decir*. In the Vulgar Latin of the Iberian Peninula, both of these verbs changed conjugation groups to become *ridire* and *dicire*. From this stage, the initial vowels dissimilated to *e* (§149d).

§89. The initial *e* (from CL *ĭ,ē*, *ĕ*, *ae*) remained *e* in Spanish:

Vulgar Latin examples from CL *ĭ* (spelled *i* in transcriptions):

ci̧rcáre > cercar	pi̧scáre > pescar
mi̧nútu > menudo	pli̧care > llegar

Vulgar Latin examples from CL *ē*:

lęntíc(u)la > lenteja	sęcúru > seguro

Vulgar Latin examples from CL *ae*:

pręcóne (CL *praecone*) > pregón
cępúlla (CL *caepullam*) > cebolla

§90. The intial VL *a* (from CL *ā*, and *ă*) remained intact:

aránea > araña	maturi(i)cáre > madrugar
cabállu > caballo	paréte > pared
cantatóre > cantor	partíre > partir
clamáre > llamar	ratióne > razón

§91. The initial VL *o* (from CL *ŭ*, *ō*, *ŏ*, *au*) gave *o* in Spanish:

Vulgar Latin examples from CL *ŭ* (spelled *u* in transcriptions):

lụcráre > lograr	sụpérbia > soberbia
nụmeráre > nombrar	sụspécta > sospecha

The change of CL *dŭbitāre* into Sp. *dudar* (instead of the expected *dodar*) has not yet been satisfactorily explained.

Vulgar Latin examples from CL *ō:*

nọmináre > nombrar	fọrmáceu > hormazo

Vulgar Latin examples from CL *ŏ:*

cọmedére > comer	cọrtícia > corteza
cọróna > corona	sọnáre > sonar

Vulgar Latin examples from CL *au:*

*au*túmnu > otoño	ra*u*báre > robar
*pau*sare > posar	

§92. The intital VL *ụ* (from CL *ū*) remained intact in Spanish:

cụráre > curar	nụb(i)láre > nublar
dụrítia > dureza	pụrítia > pureza
jụd(i)cáre > juzgar	sụdáre > sudar
mụtáre > mudar	

Final Vowels

§93. A final vowel is the unstressed vowel that is found in the last syllable of a word (fé-*ci*, amí-*cas*). It does not necessarily mean that the vowel must end the word, although such is commonly the case.

Of the groups of vowels discussed so far, the final vowel group is the weakest. The seven Vulgar Latin final vowels (*second stage*) have been reduced to only three in Spanish, and much of the time a Vulgar Latin final *e* was compeltely lost on its way to modern Spanish. The chart below shows the symmetrical development of final vowels from Classical Latin to modern Spanish:

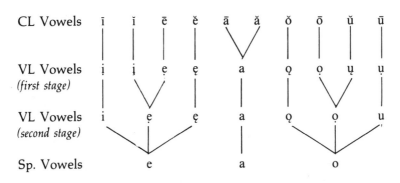

§94. The Vulgar Latin final *i* (from CL *ī*) became *e* in Spanish:

hábui > hube   pótui > pude
pósui > puse   véni >· vine

Spanish words which end in an unstressed *i*, such as *gratis, tesis, taxi,* or *cursi,* are either of learned or foreign origin.

§95a. The Vulgar Latin final *e* (from CL *ĭ, ē, ĕ*) usually disappeared during the period of Old Spanish when following any DENTAL or ALVEOLAR consonant[2] (except *t*): *-d, -l, -n, -r, -z* [dz], and *s.* In Old Spanish dialects, the final *-e* was commonly lost following other consonants as well (*noch, nuef*), but it was restored in all cases in Castilian (*noche, nueve*):

After Romance *d:*

etáte > eda*de* > edad
caritáte > carida*de* > caridad
civ(i)táte > cibda*de* > ciudad
líte > li*de* > lid
paréte > pare*de* > pared
réte > re*de* > red
salúte > salu*de* > salud
síte > se*de* > sed
tenéte > tene*de* > tened
virtute > virtu*de* > virtud

---

[2] A dental consonant is one that is articulated with the tongue against the teeth (Spanish examples include [d, t]; an alveolar consonant is one that is articulated with the tongue against the ridge behind the teeth (Spanish examples include [n, l, r, s, z]).

After *l*:

cáule > col	sále > sal
fidéle > fiel	sóle > sol
mále > mal	víle > vil

If a double *l* became final through the loss of -*e* (which was not the usual case), the *l* lost its palatal articulation: *pelle > piel, valle > val.*

After *n:*

bastóne > bastón	precóne > pregón
páne > pan	ratióne > razón
pinnóne > piñón	titióne > tizón

After *r:*

colóre > color	potére > poder
flóre > flor	rumóre > rumor
máre > mar	vendére > vender
pastóre > pastor	veníre > venir

After *s:*

cortése > cortés	revése > revés
mése > mes	trasvése > través
montése > montés	tússe > tos

After a Proto-Spanish *z:*

crúce > cruze > cruz
déce > dieze > diez
fálce > foz > hoz
lúce > luze > luz
nóce > nueze > nuez
páce > paze > paz
perdíce > perdize > perdiz

b. Due to its role as a verb ending, final *e* did not fall from verbs, even though phonetic circumstances would have allowed it to fall:[3]

---

[3] During the Middle Ages, for a time, the final *e did* fall in some verb endings, but it was finally restored to Castilian verbs in all cases. Here are some examples form the present tense: *faz, diz, sal, pon, tien, vien, quier;* and from the preterite: *fiz, pus, quis, vin.* Portuguese has retained a number of these verbs at this stage of development.

Noun	Verb
tusse > tos	tussit > tose
colore > color	coloret > colore
luce > luz	lucet > luce
sale > sal	salit > sale

c. If two consonants preceded the final *e* in Vulgar Latin, the -*e*

d(e) u*nde* > donde	pa*rte* > parte
fo*rte* > fuerte	pa*tre* > padre
le*pre* > liebre	po*nte* > puente
ma*tre* > madre	vul*t*(u)*re* > buitre
no*b*(i)*le* > noble	

d. If the consonant of the final syllable dropped, causing the final *e* to be in hiatus with the preceding vowel, the -*e* changed to a yod:

bove > buee > buey	lege > lee > ley
grege > gree > grey	rege > ree > rey

However, in the case of verbs where a consonant was lost, and the final *e* was the ending of a verb, the -*e* had to remain intact due to the requirements of the conjugation system (§173b):

legit > lee	trahit > trae
credit > cree	

§96. The Vulgar Latin final *a* (from CL *ā*, *ă*) remained in Spanish:

ám*as* > amas	fóli*a* > hoja
amíc*a* > amig*a*	língu*a* > lengua
cíli*a* > ceja	spíc*a* > espiga

§97. The Vulgar Latin final *ų* (from CL *ū*) and *o* (from CL *ŭ*, *ō*, *ŏ*) became *o* in Spanish:

Vulgar Latin example from CL *ū:*

córnu > cuerno

Vulgar Latin examples from CL *ŭ:*

lácu̦ > lago	témpu̦ > tiempo
mútu̦ > mudo	vínu̦ > vino
táuru̦ > toro	

Vulgar Latin examples from CL ō:

ámǫ > amo   plícǫ > llego
mútǫs > mudos   quandǫ > cuando

Vulgar Latin example from CL ǒ:

citǫ > cedo

Words such as *espíritu* and *tribu* are of learned origin.

Pretonic and Posttonic Internal Vowels

§98. Pretonic vowels, as the name describes, are those that are between the initial vowel and the stressed vowel; posttonic vowels are between the stressed vowel and the final vowel. Pretonic and posttonic internal vowels had already begun to fall in Vulgar Latin, as seen in the examples from the *Appendix Probi* (§9).

As Vulgar Latin evolved to Spanish, almost every unstressed internal vowel was lost, with the exception of *a*. This loss of vowels is responsible for two major features in the Spanish phonetic system. First, the loss of the posttonic internal vowel made Spanish into a language where the stress on words normally fell on the penult. Italian, on the other hand, retained most posttonic internal vowels, so its words are commonly stressed on the antepenult, as this comparative table shows:

Vulgar Latin	Italian	Spanish
álteru	áltero	ótro
dódeci	dódici	dóce
mánica	mánica	mánga
léttera	léttera	létra
nóbile	nóbile	nóble
sémita	sémita	sénda

Second, the loss of the internal unstressed vowels meant that many consonants that had never before been together were now forced to be in contact. Some of these new clusters created phonetic problems which the language had to work out one way or another, as shown below:

artíc(u)lu > artejo   lum(i)náre > lumbrar
cómp(u)to > cuento   másc(u)lu > macho
commun(i)cáre > comulgar   ráp(i)du > raudo
cúb(i)tu > codo   rét(i)na > rienda
lím(i)te > linde

The consonant resolutions shown above will be discussed as they arise in this chapter.

The chart below illustrates the general outcome of unstressed internal vowels:

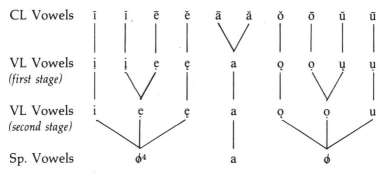

| CL Vowels | ī | ĭ | ē | ĕ | ā | ă | ŏ | ō | ŭ | ū |

VL Vowels (first stage)

VL Vowels (second stage)

Sp. Vowels ∅[4]   a   ∅

§99a. In Vulgar Latin, pretonic internal vowels (except *a*) disappeared in most cases:

lim(i)táre > lindar	ver(e)cúndia > vergüenza
lum(i)náre > lumbrar	lab(o)ráre > labrar
sem(i)táriu > sendero	hon(o)ráre > honrar
cat(e)nátu > candado	cos(u)túra > costura
comp(e)rare > comprar	pop(u)láre > poblar
litt(e)rétu > letrado	fab(u)láre > hablar
mal(e)díco > maldigo	

The few examples with a pretonic internal *a* show that it was

cal*a*mellu > caramillo   par*a*disu > paraíso

b. If there were *two* pretonic internal vowels, the one nearest the stress was lost:

cab*a*llicáre > cabalgar	hum*i*litáte > humildad
comm*u*nicáre > comulgar	ing*e*neráre > engendrar
cum*i*nitiáre > comenzar	rec*u*peráre > recobrar

§100. There are two instances, however, where the pretonic internal vowel was retained, even when the phonetic circumstances would have allowed it to drop. Both reasons are related to analogy.

First, there is the case of infinitives which must, of course, be structured on their conjugated forms. Thus, *rezbir* may be the reas-

---

[4] This symbol means 'zero'.

onable phonetic development from VL *recipíre*, but the pretonic internal *i* was forced to remain in the infinitive under analogical pressure from the conjugated forms such as *recíbo*, *recíbes*, where the *i* carries the stress.

Second, a word may not lose its pretonic interior vowel if another word in the same family is stressed on the vowel in question. For example, VL *maturáre* (Sp. *madurar*) could easily have given *madrar* were it not for the influence of the basic word *madúro*. Similarly, VL *olorósu* (Sp. *oloroso*) would have developed to *oldroso* or *orloso* were it not for the analogical pressure from *olór*.

§101. A *d* or a *g* between vowels often disappeared fairly early (§12). When they fell having been in contact with a pretonic internal *i*, the *i* could not fall and was forced to remain (many times in the form of a yod, as in the second and third examples below):

cogitáre > cuidar   tradítóre > traidor
litigáre > lidiar

§102. All posttonic interior vowels regularly fell (with the exception of a few words with a posttonic *a*:

cál(i)du > caldo	vénd(i)ga > venga
cóm(i)te > conde	vír(i)de > verde
cúb(i)tu > codo	ált(e)ru > otro
déc(i)mu > diezmo	ér(e)ma > yerma
díg(i)tu > dedo	héd(e)ra > hiedra
dóm(i)na > dueña	lítt(e)ra > letra
fém(i)na > hembra	lép(o)re > liebre
fráx(i)nu > fresno	rób(o)re > roble
gáll(i)cu > galgo	artíc(u)lu > artejo
lím(i)te > linde	cómp(u)to > cuento
mán(i)ca > manga	fáb(u)lat > habla
péd(i)cu > piezgo	másc(u)lu > macho
pós(i)tu > puesto	néb(u)la > niebla
ráp(i)du > raudo	óc(u)lu > ojo
rét(i)na > rienda	póp(u)lat > puebla
sáng(ui)ne > sangre	spec(u)lu > espejo

The posttonic internal *a* (which was usually of Greek origin) was maintained in these examples:

aspáragu > espárrago	ráphanu > rábano
órphanu > huérfano	sábana > sábana
pélagu > piélago	

§103. A few words lost their final *e* rather than losing their posttonic internal vowel. It could be that if the internal vowel had fallen, the resulting consonant clusters would have destroyed the phonetic structure of the words. It is also possible that some of the words are of learned origin:

árbore > árbol	júvene > joven
céspite > césped	márgine > margen

Vowel Inflection: The Vocalic Yod

§104. As was mentioned in §7a, in Classical Latin, if an *e* or an *i* was in hiatus, each of the vowels was the nucleus of a separate syllable (*pú-te-um*, *ál-ti-at*); but in Vulgar Latin the two vowels merged into *one* syllable, and the *e* or *i* changed into the [y] sound, called yod. [*pú-tyu*, *ál-tyat*].

The yod was unlike any other sound in the development of Spanish in that it could affect neighboring consonants or vowels in ways that no other sound could.

The yod could influence the adjacent consonants, transforming the consonants' phonetic makeup, or it could affect the preceding vowel, literally pulling it one or two steps up the vowel triangle (§3). As the language developed, some later types of yod were so strong that they could alter the neighboring consonants *and* raise the preceding vowel.

In the sections that follow, only those yods that derive from vowels and affect only the preceding vowel (or sometimes the preceding vowel *and* consonant) will be discussed.

§105. Students of Spanish have often wondered why the *-ir* verbs regularly have unusual changes in certain persons of certain conjugations where the *-ar* and *-er* verbs do not. *Dormir*, for example, shows a *u* in *durmieron*, *durmamos*, *durmiendo*, whereas *volver* has no vowel change in the same forms. The reason for this vocalic change lies in the effect exerted by a Vulgar Latin yod that existed in certain forms, and only in the *-ire* conjugation.

In the example given below, the yod raised the preceding vowel (*ę* or *ǫ*) one step up the vowel triangle (to *i* or *u* respectively). It should be remembered that these initial vowels were close in Vulgar Latin (§87):

servierunt > sirvieron	dormierunt > durmieron
servierant > sirvieran	dormierunt > durmieran
serviamus > sirvamos	dormiamus > durmamos
serviendu > sirviendo	dormiendu > durmiendo

It should be noticed that the yod was finally lost in the first person singular present subjunctive forms shown above (*serviamus* > *sirvamus*, *dormiamus* > *durmamos*). This was due to analogical pressure from the many verbs that had no yod in that form (CL *laudēmus*, *ponāmus*). The yod was not lost, however, until it had had its full phonetic effect on the preceding vowel.

§106. As a Vulgar Latin stressed ę diphthongized (§81a), a yod was created which almost always had a raising effect on the preceding initial unstressed *e:*

> ceméntu > cemientu > cimiento
> decémbre > deciembre > diciembre
> fervénte > ferviente > hirviente
> genésta > geniesta > hiniesta
> seménte > semiente > simiente

§107. The yod in a Vulgar Latin *ai* cluster first raised the *a* to *e* ([ey], the stage at which Portuguese remained), then the yod finally disappeared. The Spanish language reduced *ei* diphthongs to *e* as much as possible (other examples of this will be seen in §109):

> amai > amei > amé
> laicu > leigo > lego
> pacai > paguei > pagué
> vaika > veiga > vega

§108. In cases where a yod was created by the early loss of a *d*, the yod raised the preceding vowel. zin the examples given below, the Classical Latin word is given so that the *d*, to be lost in Vulgar Latin, may be seen.

> CL limpidum > VL lęmpiu > Sp. limpio
> CL tĕpidum > VL tępiu > Sp. tibio
> CL tŭrbidum > VL tǫrbiu > Sp. turbio

If the yod had had *no* effect, we could have expected *lempio, tebio,* and *torbio* in Spanish.

§109. The Vulgar Latin clusters *r + yod, s + yod and p + yod* usually acted in one of two different ways according to which vowel preceded them. If an *a* or an *o* (CL *ŭ*) *preceded the cluster, the yod was attracted to and combined with the preceding vowel; it mixed with a to give ai, then ei and finally e, or it mixed with the o to give oi, then óe and finally ué.* If an *e* preceded the yod, on the other hand, the yod remained where it was, but raised the preceding *e* to *i*, much like in §108, or it mixed with the preceding *e* to give *ei* which was later reduced to *e*.

r + *yod*

> a*re*a > a*i*ra > e*i*ra > era
> augu*ri*u > agu*i*ru > agoiro > agüero
> calda*ri*u > calda*i*ru > caldeiro > caldero
> co*ri*u > co*i*ru > cuero

s + *yod*

> ba*si*u > ba*i*su > beiso > beso
> caseu > ca*si*u > ca*i*su > queiso > queso
> cerasea > cera*si*a > cera*i*sa > cereiza > cereza

p + *yod*

> ca*pi*o > ca*i*po > queipo > quepo
> sa*pi*a > sa*i*pa > seipa > sepa

Here are three examples where the preceding vowel is *e:*

> cereu > cer*i*u > cirio
> pre*si*one > prisión
> mate*ri*a > made*i*ra > madera

On contact with consonants other than *r, s, p,* the yod sometimes affected both the preceding vowel *and* the preceding vowel:

> cico*ni*a > cigo*i*nia > cigüeña
> risoneu > riso*ni*u > riso*i*nio > risueño
> verecun*di*a > vergoinza > vergüenza (*d* + yod > [z])

§110. Finally, although not a yod itself, a final CL *ī* could raise a preceding vowel one step through METAPHONY (a process which causes one vowel to be influenced by another vowel in the same word; in this case, simply stated, the final CL *ī* (a high vowel) influenced the preceding *ē* to rise). Once it had its raising effect, it changed to *e* in accordance with §94:

CL fēcī > Sp. hice
CL vēnī > Sp. vine

The Wau

§111. The yod, which was built on the [i] sound, had a companion semi-vowel in Vulgar Latin known as WAU. This semi-vowel, whose name again derived from that of a Hebrew vowel, was built on the [u] sound. Its phonetic symbol is [w]. The wau has been seen in many words already: *aurum, quando, laudat,* among others.

Like the yod, the wau could exercise certain influence to raise a preceding vowel, but its workings were neither as extensive nor as vigorous as those of the yod. Its effect on consonants was minimal, as will be seen in §§124b, 125b, 126d.

Below are some examples of the workings of wau. First, the wau could raise a preceding vowel:

*egu*ale > igual

It could also switch places with the preceding consonant, as the yod did in §109, and mix with the vowel it came into contact with. These same examples were seen in §58b:

sapuī > saupi > OSp. sope
habuī > haubi > OSp. ove

As CL *vĭduam* developed, the wau raised the preceding vowel as well as changed placed with its neighboring consonant. OSp. *víuda*. Modern Spanish phonetic patterns have forced the stress to move to the *u*, thus making the original wau into a full vowel: *viúda*.

Consonants

§112. As consonants developed from Vulgar Latin to Spanish, some of them underwent very little change while others were totally transformed.

Whereas the most stable vowel from Vulgar Latin to Spanish was the one that bears the stress, the most stable consonant was the one that began a word. In the passage from Vulgar Latin to Spanish, most initial consonants were preserved intact, the notable exception being the disappearance of most initial *f*'s after the Middle Ages.

The medial consonants were the next strongest group. Vulgar

Latin unvoiced stops [p, t, k] tended not only to voice, but to become spirants [β, δ,γ] in Spanish. Vulgar Latin unvoiced double stops *pp, tt, cc,* tended to simplify to [p, t, k] whereas Vulgar Latin voiced stops [b, d, g] tended to disappear on the way to Spanish, and, in fact, most CL *g*'s already had become yods in Vulgar Latin, and these in turn had begun to fall (§11b).

When a yod was generated through a consonant cluster, the consonants usually underwent their most revolutionary changes, sometimes being altered both in manner *and* place of articulation. For example VL [kt], whose [k] element became a yod, evolved to Sp. [č], and VL [ly] became Sp. [x].

Final position was the weakest, and effectively the only Vulgar Latin final consonant that remained was the -*s*. Spanish, of course, has many more final consonants than -*s*, largely due to the fall of final *e*.

§113. The initial *d, l, m, n, p, r, t* passed into Spanish without any noticeable change:

Initial d	*Initial l*
damnare > dañar	laborare > labrar
deb(i)ta > deuda	lacte > leche
digitu > dedo	lacu > lago
dominu > dueño	lupu > lobo
duru > duro	lectu > lecho

Initial m	*Initial n*
manu > mano	nebula > niebla
minus > menos	nepta > nieta
moneta > moneda	nominare > nombrar
monte > monte	nova > nueva
mudu > mudo	nutrire > nodrir

Initial p	*Initial r*
pacat > paga	rapidu > raudo
palu > palo	ridire > reír
patre > padre	rota > rueda
pectine > peine	rotundu > redondo
porta > puerta	rugito > ruido

Initial t	
tabula > tabla	terra > tierra
tauru > toro	timere > temer
	turre > torre

§114. Since the days of Vulgar Latin, *b* and *v* were both pronounced *b* (§12), and this trait has carried through to modern Spanish:

basso > bajo	vacivu > vacío
bellu > bello	verrere > barrer
bibit > bebe	versura > basura
bonu > bueno	vinu > vino
bucca > boca	vita > vida
vacca > vaca	vult(u)re > buitre

Modern Spanish orthography favors *b-* before *a* or a back vowel, thus *barrere, basura* and *buitre* have *b-* instead of the etymological *v-*. This trend also applies internally as well: VL *advocatu* gives Sp. *abogado* and VL *aviolu* gives Sp. *abuelo*.

§115a. The VL c- before *a* or a back vowel maintained its [k] sound.[5]

capio > quepo	colore > color
capitiu > cabezo	corvu > cuervo
castellu > castilo	cuna > cuna
carru > carro	cura > cura

b. The CL *c-* before *e* or *i* was pronounced [k] in Classical Latin, but became [ts] in Vulgar Latin (§6). This latter sound remained throughout Old Spanish, but later simplified into two different spirants. In Castile, the [ts] sound simplified to a spirant based on [t], giving the modern [θ], and in the south of Spain, the [ts] simplified to the second part of the cluster [s].

celu > celo	cereu > cirio
centu > ciento	cerru > cierro
cepulla > cebolla	certu > cierto
cerasea > ceresa	cippu > cepo

In a few cases, VL *ci-* seems to have yielded *chi-* in modern Spanish. VL

In a few cases, VL *ci-* seems to have yielded *chi-* in modern Spanish. VL *cimice* has given Sp. *chinche*, probably via Mozarabic pronunciation (i.e., the pronunciation of Christian speakers of early Spanish living in Moorish occupied territory), and apparently VL *ciccu* gave Sp. *chico*.

---

[5] Sometimes the initial *c* has become *g*, as in VL *cattu* > Sp. *gato*, for example.

This brings up the problem of initial [č] in Spanish words. As the sound system developed from Vulgar Latin to Castilian, the [č] sound evolved in the *middle* of words, but did not develop at the beginning of words. Those words of Latin origin that begin with *ch-* in Castilian have come from other Hispanic dialects or languages (Galician, Portuguese, Catalan, Mallorquin), or from other languages, including Arabic, Persian, French, English and a number of Indian languages from Central and South America. Many Spanish words beginning with initial *ch-* are listed as being of 'uncertain origin' in etymological dictionaries.

§116. The initial *f-* remained through the period of Old Spanish, but finally disappeared before most vowels. There have been a number of theories suggested as to why this phenomenon took place in Castilian (whereas it did *not* in Portuguese and Catalan). The theory proposed by Menéndez Pidal is that the loss of *f-* is a direct influence of the Basque language, which has no initial *f*. When Basque speakers attempted to pronounce early Romance words beginning with *f*, they left the first sound off. The Basque country and Castile were close enough together so that a choice possibly had to be made in order to unify pronunciation: should the *f-* remain or not? The language semingly opted in favor of the Basque solution.[6]

faba > haba	fata > hada
fabulare > hablar	fervere > hervir
facie > haz	ficato > hígado
factu > hecho	fictu > hito
fastidiu > hastío	ficu > higo
filiu > hijo	fovea > hoya
fungu > hongo	fumu > humo
furnaceu > hornazo	

In very short words, where *f-* was the only consonant, it remained, contrary to the above trend: VL *fedu* > Sp. *feo*, VL *fide* > Sp. *fe*. The *f-* also usually remained before a diphthong and always before *r-*:

---

[6] Philologists call this type of phenomenon 'substrate influence'. A SUBSTRATE language is one spoken in a land before a 'conquering language' takes over. As speakers os the substrate language learn the new language, they naturally take some of their old linguistic habits with them. If these habits are widespread enough, they may influence the conquering language.

festa > fiesta
fidele > fiel
focu > fuego
fonte > fuente

fora > fuera
frenu > freno
fronte > OSp. fruente

An example where *f-* did fall before a diphthong is *ferru* > *hierro*.

§117a. Initial *g* remained [g] before *a* or a back vowel:

gallu > gallo
gaudiu > gozo

gula > gola
gutta > gota

b. Before *e*, it came to be pronounced [y], yielding *ye-* in Old Spanish, but this [y] has become all but lost in modern Spanish due to two causes. First, since the diphthong *ié* overwhelmingly derives from a *stressed* VL ę, and since an unstressed ę cannot diphthongize, Spanish tends not to allow *any* unstressed *ié* diphthongs, no matter what the source. The examples below show that the Old Spanish normal development of VL *ge-* to OSp. *ye-* was forced to be reduced to *e* in the modern language since it was unstressed:

geláre > OSp. yelar > Sp. helar
Gel(o)víra > OSp. Yelvira > Sp. Elvira
genésta > OSp. yeniesta > Sp. hiniesta
germánu > OSp. yermano > Sp. hermano
gingíva > OSp. yencía > Sp. encía

In modern Spanish, the initial *i* of *hiniesta* is due to the raising influence of the yod in the following *ie* diphthong.

c. The second reason that the initial *y* is no longer noticed is that in the examples where the initial syllable *is* stressed, the vowel of that syllable was VL ę which developed to the diphthong *ié* all by itself. The [y] developing from the original *g-* was merely absorbed into the diphthong:

gęlu > hielo

gęn(e)ru > yerno

Words beginning with *ge-* in modern Spanish are learned: *gente*,[2] *genio*, *género*.

§118a. Initial *j* before *a* retained its [y] pronunciation in Spanish:

jacere > yacer
jacet > yace

Jacobe > Yagüe
jam > ya

---

[7] CL gĕntem developed to *yente* in Old Spanish.

Jamás (from *jam magis*) came to Spanish via Old Provençal. It was the Provençal pronunciation of the *j* which developed into the modern [x] of *jamás*.

b. Before a back vowel, the *j*- developed to its modern [x] sound in a process which must have passed through these stages: [y] > [ǰ] > [ʒ] > [š] > [x]:

jogu > juego	juntu > junto
judeo > judío	jurat > jura
judex > juez	juvene > joven

Owing to the rustic nature of the implement, the word *yugo* (from VL *jugu*), which is an exception to the above trend, must be a regional development.

The [š] sound was current in Spanish in the 17th century, as shown by the French transliteration of Spanish words. *Quixote* was transliterated *Quichotte* [kišɔt] and the name of the Cid's wife (Jimena) appears as *Chimène* [šimɛn] in *Le Cid* of Corneille.

§119a. Initial *s* usually remained intact:

saltu > soto	sesu > seso
seminare > sembrar	site > sed

CL *serare* which gave Sp. *cerrar* has not yet been convincingly explained.

b. In Mozarabic dialects, initial VL *s* came to be pronounced [š] (which later developed to [x]); the following developments are attributed to Mozarabic pronunciation:

sapone > jabón	sucu > jugo
sepia > jibia	syringa > jeringa
serba > jerba	

Initial Clusters

§120. Most initial consonant clusters remained intact as Vulgar Latin developed into Spanish:

blandu > blando	frax(i)nu > fresno
blitu > bledo	fronte > frente
bracciu > brazo	pratu > prado
dracone > dragón	

VL *drappu* was altered slightly to yield Sp. *trapo*. The *gl*- cluster sometimes lost the *g* element: VL *glandine* > Sp. *landre*, VL *glattire* > Sp. *latir*, VL *glirone* > Sp. *lirón*.

§121. The initial *cl*, *fl*, and *pl* clusters usually went through a palatalization process, and all three came to be pronounced [λ]. Apparently the *l* of these clusters had been a palatal sound already in Vulgar Latin and eventually released a yod to give [kλ, fλ, pλ]; from here the *c-*, *f-*, and *p-* were lost. The spelling *ll-* was taken from the internal *ll* cluster which had the same pronunciation.

clamat > llama	plenu > lleno
clave > llave	plicare > llegar
flamma > llama	plorare > llorar
plaga > llaga	pluvia > lluvia
planu > llano	

Claro, clave, flor, plaza, plato and *pluma* show learned development.

§122. The prothetic *e* which began to precede *s* + *consonant* in Vulgar Latin (§6) universally generalized in Spanish:

schola > escuela	sposu > esposo
scribet > escribe	stat > está
scriptu > escrito	stella > estrella
scutu > escudo	strictu > estrecho

Intervocalic Single Consonants

§123. When the voiceless stops [p, t, k] were between vowels, the voiced quality of the vowels surrounding them became contageous and casued the stops to voice to [b, d, g]. This voicing had begun already in Vulgar Latin (§11). Later, the resulting voiced stops went a step farther in Spanish, becoming the voiced spirants [β, δ, γ] in most phonetic environments. The stops [p, t, k] also voiced when between vowel and *r* or *l*.

Many of the examples below illustrate that once the intervocalic stop had voiced, the unstressed vowel next to it fell: *aperire* > *aberire* > *abrir*, *bonitate* > *bonidade* > *bondad*. This evidence shows that voicing preceded syncopation.

§124a. The intervocalic *p* voiced to give a spirant *b* in Spanish:

aperire > abrir	rapu > rabo
api(c)ula > abeja	recipire > recibir
capitia > cabeza	riparia > ribera
lep(o)re > liebre	sapere > saber
lupu > lobo	superbia > soberbia
paup(e)re > pobre	

Here are some examples of voicing of *p* between a vowel and *r* or *l*:

aprigo > abrigo	capra > cabra
aprile > abril	duplare > doblar

b. If the *p* was between a semi-vowel and a vowel, the voicing was blocked:

capio > ca*i*po > queipo > quepo
sapui > sa*u*pi > OSp. sope
sapiam > sa*i*pa > seipa > sepa

c. In some cases, after the *p* voiced to *b* and the following unstressed vowel dropped, the *b* was thrown in contact with a *b*. When this happened the *b* VOCALIZED to *u*. (*Vocalize* means 'become a vowel'.) If the reader pronounces the intermediate steps in the developments (the stages with -*bd*-), he will see how close phonetically the spirant *b* is to the [w] sound.

capitále > ca*b*idale > ca*bd*al > caudal
cu*p*idítia > co*b*idicia > co*bd*icia > coudicia > codicia
lápide > la*b*ide > la*bd*e > laude
rápidu > ra*b*idu > ra*bd*o > raudo

The development of *codicia* shows that the *u* which derived from *b* was absorbed by the preceding *o* since Spanish (unlike Portuguese or Catalan) did not tolerate the *óu* diphthong. *Laude* and *raudo* show a feature which is not normal. According to §§129a and 101, we should expect the intervocalic *d* to disappear in both examples to yield the nonexistent forms *labie* and *rabio*; but since the *d* did not fall, and the *i* syncopated, the *b* was forced to vocalize.

§125a. The intervocalic *t* voiced to give the spirant *d* in Spanish. In some of the examples, once the *t* gave *d*, the final *e* was lost:

catena > cadena	materia > madera
del(i)catu > delgado	medu > miedo
litigare > lidiar	minutu > menudo

moneta > moneda   site > sed
mutare > mudar   totu > todo
pratu > prado   ver(i)tate > verdad
rete > red   vita > vida
rota > rueda   vite > vid
. seta > seda

In the case of VL *portáticu*, when the second *t* voiced to *d* and the *c* voiced to *g*, the unstressed *i* fell, and the result was *portadgo*. From this stage, the pronunciation did *not* change, but the spelling was modified to *portazgo*. (In modern Spanish, the [θ] sound voices to [δ] before a voiced consonant.)

Here are some examples of voicing of *t* between a vowel and *r*:

latrone > ladrón   putre > podre
matre > madre   utre > odre
patre > padre   vitreu > vidrio
petra > piedra

b. When between a semi-vowel and a vowel, the *t* did not voice:

au*t*umnu > otoño   cau*t*u > coto

This illustrates really how late the *au* simplified to *o*; it had to simplify only *after* the invervocalic *t* changed to *d*, otherwise we could have expected *odoño* and *codo* as developments of the above forms.

§126a. The intervocalic *c* developed in two ways according to which type of vowel followed. If an *a* or a back came after is, the *c* became the spirant *g*, but if a front vowel followed, the *c* became [θ] (or [s]), passing first through the [ts] stage. Here are some examples of a c before *a* or a back vowel:

acutu > agudo   focu > fuego
amicu > amigo   formica > hormiga
cecu > ciego   lactuca > lechuga
ciconia > cigüena   pacat > paga
commun(i)care > comulgar   plicare > llegar
del(i)catu > delgado   secare > segar
dracone > dragón   securu > seguro
ficu > higo   spica > espiga
focare > hogar   vind(i)care > vengar

These examples show the *c* between a vowel and *r*:

acreu > agrio	sacratu > sagrado
lucrare > lograr	socra > suegra
macru > magro	

b. In Vulgar Latin, if the *c* was between a semi-vowel and a mid- or back-vowel, the *c* did not voice:

au*c*a > oca	pau*c*u > poco

But is the semi-vowel *followed* the [k], voicing could still take place: *eq*ua > *yegua, aq*ua > *agua.*

c. When a front vowel followed the *c*, it evolved to the sound [dz], spelled *z*. In the 17th century, the sound unvoiced and changed to its modern [θ] or [s] depending on the dialect:

dicit > OSp. diz(e) > dice
facere > OSp. fazer > hacer
vicinu > OSp. vezino > vecino

If the front vowel following the [dz] eventually fell, the sound changed its spelling to *z* in accordance with graphic norms. If a *d* came into contact with the [dz] because of the fall of a vowel, as in the second and third examples below, the *d* assimilated into it:

lacerare > lazrar
recito > rezdo > rezo
placitu > plazdo > plazo

Similarly, if the final *e* fell following the [dz], the spelling was changed to *z*:

dece > diez	pace > paz
luce > luz	vice > vez
noce > nuez	voce > voz

§127. An *f* existed between vowels only in Latin compound words (*pro-fectu, auri-fece*) or in Greek loanwords (*raphanu, Stephanu*). This *f* usually voiced to a spirant *b*:

áfricu > ábrego	ráphanu > rábano
auríf(e)ce > OSp. orebze	Stéphanu > Esteban
cóphanu > cuévano	trífol(iu) > trébol

When it was recognized that the word was a compound, the *f* was treated as initial, and diappeared (§116): *defensa > dehesa*. A third outcome of the intervocalic *f* is sound in learned words where it naturally remains, as in the modern *defensa*.

§128. The Vulgar Latin intervocalic *b(v)* and *d* became the spirants [δ, γ] early.

a. The *b(v)* was strong and usually remained:

bibere > beber	cavare > cavar
cibu > cebo	lavare > lavar
habere > haber	neve > nieve
lib(e)rare > librar	nove > nueve
nube > nube	novu > nuevo
nub(i)lare > nublar	vivire > vivir
probare > probar	

b. However, the *b(v)* sometimes assimilated into a following back vowel and was lost. This feature began in Vulgar Latin and is seen in examples from the *Appendix Probi*.

esti*vu* > estío	su*bu*mbrariu > sombrero
ri*vu* > río	su*bu*ndare > sondar
sa*bu*cu > sauco	vaci*vu* > vacío

A few words that ended in *-iva* also lost the *v*, probably due to an analogy with the feminine forms of words such as *vacivu* > *vacío*, fem. *vacía* by analogy (instead of the expected *vaciva*, since *a* is not a back vowel):

gingiva > encía	lixiva > lejía

c. When *b(v)* was forced into contact with *d* due to the syncopation of a vowel, the *b* vocalized to *u* (as in §124c):

bíbitu > bé*b*do > béudo > beodo
civitáte > ci*b*dad > ciudad
cúbitu > co*b*do > codo
débita > de*b*da > deuda
dúbita > du*b*da > duda
lévitu > le*b*do > leudo

The change in stress (and vowel) in *beodo* has not been convincingly explained (compare with *leudo* where the natural outcome was tolerated). In the developments of *codo* and *duda*, the waus were absorbed into the preceding back vowels. In *ciudad*, the wau became a full vowel since when an *i* and a *u* are together, the

second one gets the stress, as in *viúda* and *fuíste*: thus *cibdad* >
cíudad > *ciúdad*.

§129a. The Vulgar Latin intervocalic *d* tended to drop in most
every case, as alluded to in §12:

audire > oir	limpidu > limpio
audii > oí	medulla > meollo
cadere > caer	pede > pie
crudele > cruel	rodere > roer
fastidiu > hastío	sedere > ser
fide > fe	sucidu > sucio
fidele > fiel	turbidu > turbio
fedu > feo	videre > ver
laudat > loa	

The -*d*- was also sometimes lost between a vowel and *r: catedra* >
cadera, quadraginta > *cuarenta.*

b. Syncopation of vowels apparently was earlier than the loss
of -*d*-. The examples below show that once the vowel dropped, the
-*d*- was no longer intervocalic and was thus forced to remain:

cal(i)du > caldo	sol(i)dare > soldar
ed(e)ra > hiedra	vir(i)de > verde

When the -*d*- *preceded* the vowel that was lost, and then was placed
in contact with another consonant, it merely changed its spelling
to *z* as in §125a:

jud(i)care > judgar > juzgar
ped(i)cu > piedgo > piezgo

c. Sometimes the Vulgar Latin ˙*d* remained intervocalically,
probably to that the word could retain sufficient phonetic substance:

crudu > crudo	nidu > nido
grado > grado	sudare > sudar
modu > modo	vadu > vado

§130a. The Classical Latin intervocalic *g* overwhelmingly became a yod in Vulgar Latin which was usually lost, whether it preceded a front-, mid- or back-vowel (§11b):

digitu > dedo	legis > lees
frigidu > frío	magis > más
legale > leal	magistru > maestro

The -g- was again lost much of the time between a vowel and r:
pigritia > pereza.

In some words, when an intervocalic -g- was lost before a
stressed i, the stress shifted to the more open of the two vowels in
modern Spanish:

> regína > OSp. reína > réina
> trigínta > OSp. treínta > tréinta
> vigínti > OSp. veínte > véinte

The development of rígidu to recio is not at all normal. If rigidu
(with initial i̯) had paralleled the development of frígidu (with initial
i̯), which yielded frío, we should have expected reo as its outcome. If
the word were more semantically associated with sucidu (which
gave sucio), it would be tempting to see an anology.

b. The -g- did remain in some words:

> aguriu > agüero   plaga > llaga
> agustu > agosto   rogare > rogar

§131. Other single consonants remained without change except for the single -s-, which was voiced (i.e., [z]) throughout the
Middle Ages, after which time it unvoiced to [s].

Intervocalic l   *Intervocalic r*

palu > palo   feru > fiero
pilu > pelo   pira > pera
colore > color   tauru > toro

Intervocalic m   *Intervocalic s*

fumu > humo   usu > uso
ramu > ramo   ausare > osar
timore > temor   formosu > hermoso

Intervocalic n

pinu > pino
cena > cena
lana > lana

Intervocalic Double Consonants

§132. Vulgar Latin double consonants in intervocalic position
either simplified or palatalized according to their phonetic nature.
This first section deals with those that merely simplified.

a. Intervocalic *cc* simplified to *c* [k]:

> bucca > boca   siccu > seca
> peccare > pecar   vacca > vaca
> saccu > saco

b. Intervocalic *pp* simplified to *p:*

> cippu > cepo   puppa > popa
> cuppa > copa   stuppa > estopa
> drappu > drapo

c. Intervocalic *tt* simplified to *t:*

> battire > batir   mittere > meter
> cattu > gato   sagitta > saeta
> gutta > gota   vitta > veta
> littera > letra

d. Intervocalic *ss* simplified to *s* [s]:

> grassu > graso   grossu > grueso
> passu > paso

Sometimes, however, the *-ss-* palatalized to [š] which later became [x]:

> bassu > bajo   recesso > recejo
> cessare > cejar   russu > rojo
> pássere > pájaro

The *-o* of *pájaro* is analogical with other masculine words which end in *o*; the unstressed *a* in the word dates from the formative period of Romance when there was alternation between *er* and *ar* (CL *seperare* > VL *separare*).

§133a. Intervocalic *ll* palatalized (as initial *cl*, *fl*, and *pl* did in §121) yielding the Spanish [λy].

> callare > callar   gallu > gallo
> castẹllu > castillo   mọllu > muelle
> cẹllu > cilla   pụllu > pollo
> cepụlla > cebolla   valle > valle
> cọllu > cuello   vịllu > vello
> fọlle > fuelle

As the above examples show, the yod released by the palatal *l* did

not affect the preceding vowel in any way, except as noted pre-
viously (§81b*i*) about such words as *castillo* and *cilla*.

b. If a palatal *l* came into syllable- or word-final position, it lost
its palatal nature (see also §95a in the explanation of *l*):

foll(i)care > holgar	mill(e) > mil
gall(i)cu > galgo	pell(e) > piel

c. Intervocalic *ffl* and *fl* also developed to a palatal *l*: *ll*.[8]

afflare > hallar	suflare > sollar

§134. Like the intervocalic *ll*, the Vulgar Latin intervocalic *nn*
also palatalized in Spanish to *ñ:*

annu > año	pinna > piña
canna > caña	pannu > paño
grunnire > gruñir	

The *m* of the -*mn*- cluster apparently assimilated very early to
the *n* so that the cluster could develop as a normal -*nn*- cluster:

autumnu > otoño	dom(i)nu > dueño
damnu > daño	calumnia > caloña

§135a. When a Vulgar Latin intervocalic *sc* preceded a front
vowel, the result in Old Spanish was [ts], spelled *ç*. This simplified
in the sixteenth century to its modern outcome [θ] or [s], depending on the dialect:

crescere > OSp. creçer > crecer
miscere > OSp. meçer > mecer
pascere > OSp. paçer > pacer

b. In cases where a final *e* had fallen following the OSp. *ç*, its
spelling changed to *z*:

fasce > OSp. façe > haz
pisce > OSp. peçe > pez

---

[8] If the *fl* followed a consonant, it could not develop as it would in
intervocalic position, yet it still succeeded in developing into a palatal
sound, the [č], which is even a more complicated development than the
palatal *l*: *inflare > hinchar*. Similarly, a consonant before *pl* caused it to
develop to [č] as well: *implere > henchir, amplu > ancho*. These examples
parallel the Portuguese development of initial *fl* and *pl*: *flamma > Ptg.
chama; plaga > Ptg. chaga*.

Single Consonant + Vocalic Yod

§136. In early Vulgar Latin (§13), the *t* + *yod* and the *c* + *yod* clusters between vowels (or between *r* and a vowel) were pronounced first [ty] and [ky]; later, both came to be pronounced [ts], the yod having expended itself to make the [s] sound. Since the yod was lost so early, it had no raising effect on the preceding vowel in Spanish, as the examples below demonstrate. In Old Spanish, the Vulgar Latin [ts] voiced to [dz], which later unvoiced to its modern Spanish result [θ] or [s].

durȷtia > dureza	coracea > coraza
fọrtia > fuerza	facie > haz
matea > maza	furnaceu > hornazo
platea > plaza	minacea > (a)menaza
purȷtia > pureza	pellịcea > pelliza
puṭeu > pozo	post cọcceu > pescuezo

§137. The yod of the *b(v)*, *d*, *g* + *yod* clusters was never, as a rule, assimilated into any of the three consonants (as it was in §136 above), and thus was able to raise the preceding vowel. This yod was not of the strongest type; it usually raised a preceding back vowel, sometimes raised a preceding front vowel, but never raised a preceding *a*. Vulgar Latin vowel quality is shown in the examples below where the effects of raising would ordinarily not be apparent through usual orthography.

a. The *b(v)* + *yod* cluster remained intact most of the time:

aleviare > aliviar	plụvia > lluvia
levianu > liviano	rabia > rabia
nọviu > novio	

b. Sometimes the *b(v)* disappeared, leaving only the yod:

fọvea > hoya	rubeu > royo
habea > haya	

§138a. The *d* + *yod* cluster tended to lose its initial element in most cases, leaving only the yod:

adiutare > ayudar	pọdiu > poyo
họdie > hoy	sẹdea > OSp. seya > sea

The yod was lost in *seya* to avoid the *ei* cluster.

b. When the *d* + *yod* was no longer intervocalic, or (seemingly) when it followed a CL *u*, the *d* + *yod* developed to [dz] which later simplified to [θ] or [s]:

acudiare > aguzar   verecundia > vergüenza
gaudiare > gozar   virdia > berza

§139. The *g* + *yod* cluster always lost its initial element, but the yod remained. The *g* was lost because it first became a yod itself (§12), and the two yods merely merged:

arrugiu > arroyo   fugio > huyo
corregia > correya > correa   Legione > Leyón > León
exagiu > ensayo

The yods were lost in *correya* and *Leyón* again to avoid ther *ei* cluster. In *ensayo* there was an erroneous confusion of prefixes (§157a).

§140. The *n* + *yod* cluster and the *gn* cluster both gave [ñy] in Spanish, and both occasionally raised the preceding vowel:

a. Here are some examples with *n* + *yod*:

aranea > araña   ingeniu > engeño
cụnea > cuña   pinea > piña
extraneu > extraño   seniore > señor
Hispania > España

b. The *gn* cluster apparently developed as follows: [gn] > [yn] > [ñy]:

ligna > leña   stagnu > estaño
pụgnu > puño   tam magnu > tamaño
signa > seña

The words *reinar* (from *regnare*) and *reino* (from *regnu*), stunted in their development due to the influence of *rey*, attest the second stage in the phonetic evolution of this cluster.

Yod Clusters That Yielded the *jota*

§141. The *l* + *yod* cluster, which developed to the *jota* in Spanish, had a more complex development than any yod cluster discussed so far. It probably evolved in this way: [λy] > [ʒ] > [ʒ] > [š] > [x]. With almost all of its energy used up in the transformation of the consonant, the yod only had a minimal effect on the raising of the vowels; only *hoja* and *mujer* below show raised vowels:

alienu > ajeno	fọlia > hoja
aliu > ajo	mụliere > mujer
cịliu > cejo	palea > paja
consịliu > consejo	tịliu > tejo
fịliu > hijo	

If the *l* + yod was not intervocalic, it could not develop as above. After a consonant, as the following example shows, it developed to [č]: *cocleare* > *cuchara*.

§142a. The *c'l* and *g'l* clusters (an apostrophe indicates that a Latin vowel has fallen; in the examples below, the vowel that *is to* fall is shown between parentheses) developed as the *l* + *yod* clusters did. Once the unstressed vowel fell, the *c* and the *g* became yods and both clusters yielded [λy]. This new cluster became [λy] and joined the *l* + *yod* development. Again, this cluster only rarely affected the preceding vowel (as in *ojo* below). The initial *ẹ* of *gen(u)culu* was not raised because of the yod, but rather was probably influenced by the initial *g*.

api*c*(u)*l*a > abeja	lenti*c*(u)*l*a > lenteja
arti*c*(u)*l*u > artejo	ọ*c*(u)*l*u > ojo
cuni*c*(u)*l*u > conejo	cua*g*(u)*l*u > cuajo
genu*c*(u)*l*u > hinojo	re*g*(u)*l*a > reja
ori*c*(u)*l*a > oreja	te*g*(u)*l*la > teja

If *mirac(u)lu* and *sec(u)lu* had developed in the normal way, they would have become *mirajo* and *sejo*. Since they were both part of the conservatively developing ecclesiastic vocabulary, they became *milagro* (OSp. *miraglo* [§151a]) and *siglo*.

b. If an *l*, an *n* or an *s* preceded these clusters, they usually developed to [č]:[9]

cal*c*(u)*l*u > cacho	man*c*(u)*l*a > mancha
cin*g*(u)*l*u > cincho	mas*c*(u)*l*u > macho
con*c*(u)*l*a > concha	trun*c*(u)*l*u > troncho

---

[9] *N'gl* shows a few curious developments: *spong(u)la* > *esponja* shows intervocalic development of *g'l*; *sing(u)los* > *sendos* shows a change of *l* to *d*; *singulariu* > *señero*, *ung(u)la* > *uña* show a change to *ñ*. *S'cl* also has a few aberrant developments: *musc(u)lu* > *muslo* shows loss of *c*, and *mesc(u)lare* > *mezclar* is semi-learned.

The Latin *tl* cluster, because it was so uncommon, sometimes was transformed into *cl* in Vulgar Latin, and this *cl* developed normally. The *Appendix Probi* corrects: *vetulus non veclus*.

CL rotulare > VL roclare > Sp. (ar)rojar
CL vetulum > VL vęclu > Sp. viejo

Viejo presents an unsolved problem: why did the *ę* diphthongize when the yod was supposed to prevent diphthongization? We should have expected *vejo*. It is usually stated that *viejo* is a borrowing from Aragonese (where such diphthongs freely occur), yet it seems unlikely that such a common core word could be a borrowing.

For another outcome of the *tl* cluster, see §151b.

§143. The Vulgar Latin [ks], which also yielded *jota* in Spanish, gave rise to a powerful yod which was strong enough to raise a preceding *a* to *e*. Up to now, no yod had been able to raise a preceding *a*. The development of this cluster appears to have been: [ks] >[ys] > [sy] > [š] > [x].

axe > eje   laxus > lejos
cǫxo > cojo   lịxiva > lejía
dịxi > dije   mataxa > madeja
exemplu > ejemplo   maxịlla > mejilla
laxare > dejar   taxone > tejón

It is odd that *lejía* did not become *lijía*. The initial *d* of *dejar* is an unresolved Hispanic question. French and Italian retain the original *l* (*laisser, lasciare*), while Spanish shows the initial *d*, and Portuguese shows two variants with *deixar* in the modern language and *leixar* in older Portuguese.

When the *i* of *fraxinu* fell, the *x* was no longer intervocalic. The yod that developed in this word when *x* became [ys] raised the *a* to *e*, then it disappeared, leaving the *s* intact: *fraxinu > fresno*.

The CT Cluster

§144a. The *-ct-* cluster, which developed to [č] in Spanish, also gave rise to a very powerful yod that could raise *a* to *e*. The development of the [kt] seems to have been [kt] > [ky] > [yty] > [č]:

despęctu > despecho	nǫcte > noche
dįctu > dicho	pęctu > pecho
dųctu > ducho	propfęctu > provecho
factu > hecho	strįctu > estrecho
iactare > echar	tęctu > techo
lacte > leche	trųcta > trucha
lactuca > lechuga	verbactu > barbecho

As powerful as this yod was, it sometimes did (*dicho*) and sometimes did not (*estrecho*) raise a Vulgar Latin *į* to Sp. *i*. *Iactare* did not develop to *yechar* for the reasons stated in §117b.

b. When the *-ct-* followed vowels at the extreme end of the vowel triangle (the *į* and the *ų*), the yod was absorbed or lost, leaving the *t* intact:

exsųctu > enjuto	frįctu > frito
fįctu > hito	frųctu > fruto

c. In contact with a consonant, the *-ct-* cluster could not develop as it would between vowels. The *c* fell in Vulgar Latin (§15e), and was sometimes able to raise the preceding vowel:

jųn(c)tu > junto	pųn(c)tu > punto

Pectine offers an interesting case. When the unstressed vowel fell, leaving *pect'ne*, the *-ct-* cluster, although less constricted than when the *n* preceded it, could still not develop fully. The *c* became yod and the *t* fell: *pect'ne* > *peine* (the *i* of *peine* was retained here extraordinarily in order to avoid an unfortunate homonym).

The word *collacteu* presents another interesting development, showing how two conflicting clusters developed. The *-ct-* cluster (*collacteu*) would normally yield [č], but the *t* + *yod* cluster (*collacteu*) developed to [ts] before this change was possible; the *c* could do nothing else but assimilate to the *t* and fall: *collacteu* > *collactso* > *collatso* > *collazo*.

Clusters with L

§145. When a VL *l* preceded a consonant, much of the time it vocalized to *u*, which is a close acoustic relative to *l*. When *a* preceded the *l*, the cluster developed in this way: [al] > [au] > [o]. When *u* preceded the *l*, the cluster passed through these stages: [ul] > [uu] > [u]:

altariu > otero	falce > hoz
alt(e)ru > otro	falcino > hocino
calce > coz	saltu > soto
culm(i)ne > cumbre	talpa > topo

If *al* came into contact with a consonant owing to the loss of a vowel, the cluster yielded *au: cal(i)ce > calce > cauce, sal(i)ce > salce > sauce. Topo* shows an unusual gender change.

§146. The *-ul't-* cluster acted in a different way from the way it did above. The *l*, instead of changing into a wau (in which case it would be absorbed by the preceding *u*), changed to a yod by dissimilation (§149d). The yod then acted on the *t* to form [č], and raised the *u* to *u*. Here is the apparent development of the cluster: [ult] > [uyt] > [uty] > [uč].

ascultare > escuchar	multu > mucho
cultello > cuchillo	

When the *-ult-* cluster was followed by a consonant, as in *vul-t're*, it could not evolve as above. Its evolution was arrested at the second step shown above: *vúlture > vúlt're > búitre*. There was then a normal shift in stress to the *i* giving Sp. *buitre. Muy* (from *mult[u]*) also shows arrested development at the second step.

Final Consonants

§147a. Most Vulgar Latin final consonants were lost along the way to Spanish:

Final d	*Final t*
ad > a	aut > o
aliquod > algo	dicit > dice
illud > ello	laudat > loa
istud > esto	stat > está

Final c	*Final b*
dic > di	sub > OSp. so
nec > ni	
sic > sí	

Nec (with its *ę*) ordinarily would have developed to *ne*, but the form *ni* is doubtless analogical with other short words ending in *-i* such as *sí*.

b. The final *m* was already lost in Vulgar Latin (§10). The final *m* in monosyllabic words changed to *n*, most likely because Spanish had no final BILABIAL consonant (*Bilabial* means 'articulated with the two lips.'):

cụm > con   tam > tan
quẹm > quien

This lack of final *m* accounts for the Spanish *-n* in borrowings such as *Jerusalén, Adán,* and *Belén.*

§148a. Vulgar Latin final *l, r,* and *x* did not fall:

Final *l*	Final *r*	Final *x*
fẹl > hiel	inter > entre	sẹx > seis
mẹl > miel	quattuor > cuatro	
	sẹmper > siempre	

The final *r* in the above examples switched places with the preceding vowel. The [ks] of *sẹx* changed its [k] element into a yod which prevented the diphthongization of the preceding vowel: [seks] > [seys]. The *x* when intervocalic would develop to [č], of course, but in *sex*, we have a case of the survival of *final x*, and its development was thus stunted at the first stage of development as seen in §143 above.

b. Vulgar Latin final *s* universally remained in verb forms as well as in noun and adjective plurals:

fab(u)las > hablas   patres > padres
formosos > hermosos

Old Spanish carried over some third declension neuter *singular* forms that ended in *s* (§21a), but the language finally did not tolerate singular forms with final *s*, thus the etymological *s* was lost:

Singular

corpus > OSp. cuerpos > cuerpo
opus > OSp. huebos (§153b)
pectus > OSp. pechos > pecho
tempus > OSp. tiempos > tiempo

Dissimilation, Assimilation and Metathesis

§149. DISSIMILATION is the process whereby, in a word with two like sounds, one of the two sounds is altered or eliminated.

a. As the Spanish language developed, it did not usually allow two *r*'s, two *l*'s or two nasals in the same word, and usually changed the manner of articulation of the second of the two sounds, although sometimes the first was altered.

r - *r* > *r* - *l*	*n* - *n* > *l* - *n*, *n* - *l*, *n* - *r*
a*r*bo*re* > á*r*bo*l*	de i*n* a*n*te > de*l*a*n*te
ca*r*ce*re* > cá*r*ce*l*	i*n*g(ui)*ne* > i*n*g*l*e
ma*r*mo*re* > má*r*mo*l*	hispa*n*io*ne* > españo*l*
robo*re* > rob*l*e	sa*n*g(ui)*ne* > sa*n*g*r*e
sterco*l*re > estiérco*l*	

l - *l* > *r* - *l*, *l* - *r*	*n* - *m* > *l* - m, *r* - m
ca*l*ame*ll*u > ca*r*ami*ll*o	a*n*(i)*m*a > a*l*ma
*l*oca*l*e > *l*uga*r*	mi*n*(i)*m*are > me*r*mar

b. When a vowel syncopated between an *m* and an *n*, the *n* dissimilated to *r* most of the time, then a *b* was generated between the two to make the new cluster pronounceable and also to conserve the *r* as a single tap. (without the *b*, the *r* would have to be pronounced as a multiple trill, as in *honra*.)

costu*m*(i)*ne* > costu*mbr*e lu*m*(i)*ne* > lu*mbr*e
cul*m*(i)*ne* > cu*m*bre no*m*(i)*ne* > no*mbr*e
fe*m*(i)*na* > he*mbr*a se*m*(i)*n*are > se*mbr*ar
ho*m*(i)*ne* > ho*mbr*e

In *communicare*, an ecclesiastic word, since there was no syncopation between *m* and *n* (§99b), the *n* dissimilated to *l*: *commun(i)care* > *comulgar*.

c. Another type of dissimilation was very strong, causing one of the consonants to disappear completely instead of merely changing its point of articulation.

*b*o*b*e > *b*oe > buey
pro*pr*iu > propio
tra*s*ve*s*e > través
trem(u)lare > trem'lare > *tr*emb*l*are > temb*l*ar

In the last example, it was not until the *b* developed that the dissimilation took place. It is a case of dissimilation of two *muta cum liquida* clusters.

d. Occasionally vowels also dissimilated, but not with the pattern of predictably that consonants show:

dịcire > decir	rịdire > reír
formọsu > hermoso	verrere > barrer
rotụndu > redondo	vịcino > vecino

§150a. Assimilation (the opposite of *dissimilation*) is the process where two unlike sounds in a given word become the same. *Full assimilation* is where one sounds grows to be identical with another sound in the same word; one example of this is *il(i)cina > encina* (*l - n > n - n*).

b. *Partial* assimilation is where one sound, put in contact with another due to the syncopation of a vowel or the loss of a consonant, has to adjust its point of articulation to match that of the following consonant:

com(i)te > conde	lim(i)tare > lindar
com(pu)tare > contar	sem(i)ta > senda
ven(di)care > vengar (n = [ŋ])	

c. Sometimes a consonant cannot properly adjust to the point of articulation of the following consonant and instead, a third consonant is generated between the two (similar to §149b above):

hum(e)ru > hombro	trem(u)lare > temblar
pon(e)ré > pondré	val(e)ré > valdré
sal(i)ré > saldré	ven(i)ré > vendré
ten(e)ré > tendré	

If the first consonant is alveolar (*l, n*) a *d* is generated; if it is bilabial (*m*), a *b* is generated.

§151a. Metathesis is the process where one or two sounds change position. When only one consonant changes place in a word (*crepare > quebrar*), it is called *simple metathesis*. When *two* consonants switch places with each other (*animalia > alimaña*), it is called *reciprocal metathesis*.

animalia > alimaña	oblitare > olvidar
crepare > quebrar	maturicare > madrugar
integrare > entregar	parabola > palabra
mirac(u)lu > milagro	peric(u)lu > peligro

b. After a vowel has syncopated, awkward consonant clusters are sometimes created. Metathesis is often the easiest way to resolve these clusters:

ac(e)re > arce   col(o)rare > corlar
capit(u)lu > cabildo   gen(e)ru > yerno
cat(e)natu > candado   ret(i)na > rienda
spat(u)lu > espalda   tit(u)lare > tildar
ten(e)ru > tierno   ven(e)ris > viernes

Capit(u)lu, spat(u)lu and *tit(u)lare* show a different solution to the *t'l* cluster from the one in §142c. These (due to the voicing of *t*) obviously show a later syncopation.

c. There was a special metathesis in verbs ending in *ficare*. The *f* ffirst voices to *b*, then vocalizes to *u*, and at *that* point the metathesis takes place.

pacif(i)care > pacibgar > paciugare > (a)paciguar
santif(i)care > santibgar > santiugar > santiguar

d. VL *fábr(i)ca* deserves special mention. When the unstressed vowel dropped, the word was placed in a phonetic conflict which was not resolved until until metathesis affected it twice and the *b* vocalized to *u*:

fabr(i)ca > fabrga > frauga > fragua

This simplified survey of the historical development of speech sounds has been prepared to give the novice an indication of what happened in the evolution of Spanish phonology. This chapter also lays the groundwork for some of the important points in the final chapter dealing with morphology.

3

Form Change Through Time:
Historical Morphology

The Development of Nouns

§152a. In Vulgar Latin, nouns had two distinct cases, the nominative and the accusative (§§27-30). When the Vulgar Latin of Hispania evolved into Old Spanish, however, the nominative case was lost in almost every case, and the accusative case—which was much more common than the nominative, given its diversified role in Vulgar Latin—was overwhelmingly the only one to survive.

b. Here are some examples from the Vulgar Latin first declension. They include a number of forms that the Vulgar Latin first declension inherited from different Classical Latin sources; for example, Classical Latin second declension neuter plurals (*pira, vota*, §28c), Classical Latin third declension nouns made into the first declension by addition of a diminutive suffix (*apic(u)la, oric-(u)la*, §33c), fourth declension nouns with diminutive suffixes (*acuc-(u)la, capitia*, §77b), and fifth declension nouns (*dia, materia* §32):

acuc(u)la > aguja	oric(u)la > oreja
apic(u)la > abeja	perna > pierna
capitia > cabeza	pira > pera
cepulla > cebolla	porta > puerta
dia > día	vota > boda
materia > madera	

c. The following examples are from the Vulgar Latin second

declension. They include some masculine forms inherited from the Classical Latin second declension neuter (*balneu, collu, vinu,* §28b) and some forms from the fourth declension (*cornu, frax(i)nu, manu* §31):

amicu > amigo	dom(i)nu > dueño
balneu > baño	filiu > hijo
castellu > castillo	frax(i)nu > fresno
collu > cuello	manu > mano
cornu > cuerno	vinu > vino

d. The examples below are from the Vulgar Latin third declension. The sampling includes forms that derived from the Vulgar Latin fifth declension (*facie, fide,* §32):

calle > calle	hom(i)ne > hombre
carcere > cárcel	lacte > leche
civ(i)tate > ciudad	latrone > ladrón
dolore > dolor	mare > mar
facie > haz	parete > pared
fide > fe	ratione > razón
fonte > fuente	rege > rey

§153a. The third declension, as usual, offers more complications than the other ones. Many third declension nouns which served for both masculine and feminine genders soon added an analogical -*a* to the feminine in Old Spanish to differentiate the genders; this differentiation has remained into the modern language:

hispanione > OSp. español *f* > española
infante > OSp. infante *f* > infanta
latrone > OSp. ladrón *f* > ladrona
parente > OSp. pariente *f* > parienta
pastore > OSp. pastor *f* > pastora
seniore > OSp. señor *f* > señora

b. Some third declension neuters created a problem because their accusative form ended in -*s* in the singular (§21a). This final *s* carried through Vulgar Latin and into Old Spanish where these forms are seen:

corpus (*sing.*) > OSp. cuerpos (*sing.*)
pectus (*sing.*) > OSp. pechos (*sing.*)
opus (*sing.*) > OSp. huebos (*sing.*)
tempus (*sing.*) > OSp. tiempos (*sing.*)

These were eventually 'logically' regarded as plurals in Old Spanish, and analogical singulars, without *-s*, were created: *cuerpo*, *pecho, tiempo* (§148b). *Huebos* was not continued. The *h-* of *huebos*, it might be mentioned in passing, is of course not etymological. It was placed before a vocalic *u* in Old Spanish as an orthographioc signal to distinguish the vowel *u* from the consonant *v*, both of which were spelled *u*; without the *h*, *huebos* might have been read as *vebos* otherwise. Other examples which show an added orthographic *h-* are: *orphanu* > *huérfano, ossu* > *hueso, ovu* > *huevo*.

c. Those Vulgar Latin third declension neuter accusative forms that ended in a consonant (other than *-s*) were rebuilt with final *-e*, by analogy with the commoner third declension masculine and feminine nouns with final *-e* in Vulgar Latin (such as VL acc. *hom-(i)ne, civ(i)tate, dolore, ratione, monte*). The first five Vulgar Latin forms below appear to be built on the model of *hom(i)ne*.

> CL culmen > VL culm(i)ne > Sp. cumbre
> CL examen > VL exam(i)ne > Sp. enjambre
> CL inguen > VL ing(ui)ne > Sp. ingle
> CL nomen > VL nom(i)ne > Sp. nombre
> CL piper > VL pib(e)re > Sp. pebre
> CL sulphur > VL sulph(u)re > Sp. (a)zufre

§149b describes how *-m(i)ne* of some of the above examples became *-mbre*. Ther *n - n* of *inguine* dissimilated to *n - l* (§149a).

§154. The fourth and fifth declensions have left no direct trace through normal development since they both changed declension group in Vulgar Latin, but the Spanish language has taken some learned fourth and fifth declension forms from Classical Latin:

> *Fourth Declension*
>
> espíritu
> tribu
>
> *Fifth Declension*
>
> especie
> serie
> superficie

§155a. The plural form of nouns usually offered no complications since it was almost always the direct development of the Vulgar Latin accusative plural:

amicos > amigos	capitias > cabezas
calles > calles	civ(i)tates > ciudades
dom(i)nos > dueños	portas > puertas
filios > hijos	rationes > razones
pernas > piernas	ver(i)tates > verdades

b. Those neuter singulars which had Classical Latin plurals in
-a, took analogical plurals in Spanish ending in -os and -es:

CL balneum, pl. balnea > Sp. baño, baños
CL collum, pl. colla > Sp. cuello, cuellos
CL cornu, pl. cornua > Sp. cuerno, cuernos
CL mare, pl. maria > Sp. mar, mares
CL vinum, pl. vina > Sp. vino, vinos

c. Second declension neuter plurals that became Vulgar Latin
first declension singulars (§28c), built analogical plurals by adding
-s:

VL cilia > Sp.   ceja, pl. cejas
VL festa >   Sp. fiesta, pl. fiestas
VL folia > Sp.   hoja, pl. hojas
VL ligna > Sp.   leña, pl. leñas
VL pira > Sp.   pera, pl. peras
VL signa > Sp.   seña, pl. señas
VL vascella > Sp.   vajilla, pl. vajilllas
VL vota > Sp.   boda, pl. bodas

Vestiges of Latin Cases Other Than the Accusative

§156. Whereas the vast majority of Spanish nouns have evolved
from the accusative case of Vulgar Latin, a few fossilized remains
from other cases have managed to survive in a Spanish.

a. The nominative has been preserved in pronouns associated
with the nominative as well as in a few names:

ego > yo	tu > tú
il(le) > él	Car(o)lus > Carlos
ipse > ese	Deus > Dios
iste > este	Marcus > Marcos

There are a number of learned nominatives, of course, which were
taken in fairly recent times directly from Classical Latin, such as
ábdomen, carácter, cráter, crisis, espécimen, régimen, tórax.

b. The genitive is seen in fossilized forms in a few words, most notably in the days of the week:

> (dies) martis [= Mars' day] > martes
> (dies) jovis [= Jupiter's day] > jueves
> (dies) veneris [= Venus' day] > viernes

By analogy with the above third declension forms ending in -*is*, the first declension *(dies) lunae* [= Moon's day] became *lunis* which gave Sp. *lunes.* The second declension *(dies) mercuri* [= Mercury's day] became *mercuriis* which gave *miércoles* in Spanish (with dissimilation *r* - *r* to *r* - *l*). (*Sábado* comes from VL *sábbatu* and *domingo* comes from *(dies) domin(i)cus.*

Other vestiges of the genitive (shown in italics) are seen in:

> comite *stabuli* > 'count of the stable' > condestable
> filiu *ecclesiae* 'son of the church' > feligrés
> *pedis* ungula 'nail of the foot' > pesuña
> forum *judicum* 'court of the judges' > *Fuero Juzgo*
> Campus *Gothorum* 'Field of the Goths' > Toro

c. The only remains of the Latin dative in Spanish are found in the development of the dative pronouns: *(il)lī* > *le, (il)līs* > *les.*

d. There are a few vestiges of the ablative case fossilized in a small number of Spanish words:

> CL hāc horā > OSp. agora[1]
> CL hōc annō > Sp. hogaño
> CL locō > Sp. luego
> CL quōmodo > Sp. como

Prefixes and Suffixes

§157a. There was sometimes a confusion or accumulation of prefixes as Vulgar Latin developed into Spanish. The first example shows that the prefix *ex-* was substituted for *a(b)s-*:

> a(b)scondere > esconder
> ascultare > escuchar

The following examples reveal that *in-* attached itself to the words.

---

[1] Modern Spanish *ahora* derived from *ad horam.*

esagiu > in(e)xagiu > ensayo
exam(i)ne > in(e)xam(i)ne > enjambre
exemplu > in(e)xemplu > OSp. enxiemplo

In this example, the prefix *in-* mixed with the initial *i*:

hibernu > inbernu > invierno

b. A few suffixes were occasionally confused, the more common ones overpowering the less common ones:

capellanu (+ -ane) > capellán
foll(i)catianu (+ -ane) > holgazán
tosoria (+ -aria) > tijera
certitudine (+ -um[i]ne) > certidumbre
cos(ue)tudine (+ -um[i]ne) > costumbre
mans(u)etudine(+ -um[i]ne) > mansebumbre
multitudine(+ -um[i]ne) > muchedumbre

The Latin suffix *-aticu* developed normally to *-azgo* (§125a), as in *afflaticu > hallazgo, portaticu > portazgo*. But the French result, *-age*, was also borrowed by Spanish as *-aje*, as shown in these loanwords: *garaje, portaje, salvaje, viaje*. The *i* of *tijera* appears to be due to the infulence of the *i* of VL *cisoriu* 'scissors'.

Articles

§158a. The Spanish definite articles derive from the Latin demonstratives *ille, illa, illud*,[2] which had already begun to be used in the function of definite articles in Vulgar Latin (§34). The singular articles have their origin in the nomintaive forms of these demonstratives, while the plural articles were taken from the accusative forms. (The same alternation—nominative used in the singular and accusative in the plural—will be seen in the Spanish demonstratives, §162). In the Vulgar Latin of Hispania, the demonstratives used as articles lost one syllable in every form, usually the *il-*, except in the masculine singular:

CL ille > VL il > Sp. el
CL illōs > VL los > Sp. los
CL illa > VL la > Sp. la

---

[2] It should be noticed that the neuter form (*illud*) was retained, contrary to the tendency to drop neuters.

CL illas > VL las > Sp. las
CL illud > VL lu > Sp. lo

b. A few words should be said about the feminine article *el* (as in *el águila, el agua, el alma*); it did not derive from the second syllable of *illa*, but from the first, as the examples below show:

illa aqua (= [ilákwa]) > el agua
illa aquila (= [ilákwila]) > el águila
illa anima (= [ilánima]) > el alma

Because of the fusion of the two *a*'s, the initial *i* of *illa* was forced to remain. In Old Spanish, *el* was used before any initial *a*, stressed or not, but gradually it came to be used only before a stressed *a*-.

§159. The indefinite articles which began to come into existence in Vulgar Latin (§34), remained in Spanish:

unu > un   una > una
unos > unos   unas > unas

Unu lost its last syllable due to its PROCLITIC nature (that is, its use as an unstressed word which forms a unit with the following word). When it is no longer proclitic, the lost syllable returns: *Tengo* un *coche bueno pero él tiene* uno *mejor.*

Adjectives

§160. The accusative forms of Vulgar Latin adjectives evolved into Spanish adjectives without complications.

a. The first group of adjectives, based on the first and second declensions, maintains the differences between masculine and feminine genders in its forms (§35a):

bibitu,-a > beodo,-a   delicatu,-a > delgado,-a
bonu,-a > bueno,-a   duru,-a > duro,-a
extraneu,-a > extraño,-a   limpidu,-a > limpio,-a
fedu,-a (CL foedam) > feo,-a mutu,-a> mudo,-a
formosu,-a > hermoso,-a   securu,-a > seguro,-a
grossu,-a > grueso,-a   strictu,-a > estrecho,-a
integru,-a > entero,-a   tepida > tibio,-a

b. The second group of adjectives, based on the third declension, does not usually show a difference in gender:

alegre (CL *alacrem)* > alegre	grande > grande
crudele > cruel	paup(e)re > pobre
equale > igual	regale > real
fidele > fiel	stab(i)le > estable
felice > feliz	turpe > torpe
forte > fuerte	vir(i)de > verde

Before a noun, *grande* becomes *gran*, a relic of Old Spanish *grant*. The third declension adjectives ending in *-or* in Old Spanish began to take an analogical femenine *-a* around 1300, much as in §153a. Examples include *entendedora, habladora*.

c. The adjective *mismo* seems to require a short, simplified, section to itself. In Classical Latin, to say 'I, myself', all that was needed was to attach the particle *-met* to the pronoun: *egomet*. To be more emphatic, the adjective *ipse* 'self' was added: *egomet ipse*. With the passage of time, the original emphasis wore off this construction, so *ipse* was made into a superlative: *egomet ipsissimus*. This construction became so well used that *metipsíssimus* could be used by itself. (In Classical Latin, *-met* could not be separated from the pronoun to which it was attached.) In Vulgar Latin, the form developed to something like this: *medissíssimu*. It was at this point that HAPLOLOGY took place. Haplology, related to dissimilation, is the process whereby two like syllables (*iss-iss* in this case) are reduced to one, yielding *medis(i)mu* in this word. It developed to *medesmo* (*-iss(i)mu* contained a short *i* in Latin), then to *mesmo*, which is the most common form of the word through the era of Cervantes and is also the current form in Portuguese. So far, everything has been rather easy to explain. It is the bizarre change from *mesmo* to *mismo* which has not yet been satisfactorily resolved.

§161a. The comparative and superlative systems did not basically change since Vulgar Latin times (§37):

> magis fidele > más fiel
> magis felice > más feliz
> magis securu > más seguro
> il magis fidele > el más fiel
> la magis felice > la más feliz
> las magis securas > las más seguras

Magis evolved to *mais* in Old Spanish. Certainly its common proclitic use helped to simplify it to *más*.

. b. The irregular comparatives (§38) developed normally:

maiore > mayor   minore > menor
meliore > mejor   peiore > peor

It should be noticed that these particular third declension words ending in *-or* did not add an analogical *-a* to make a feminine form (contrary to §§153a, 160b).

Demonstratives

§162. The demonstratives that remained in Vulgar Latin (§39ab) were continued into Spanish. It was the nominative form that gave rise to the Spanish singular forms, but it was the accusative form that became the Spanish plural.

Singular (= nom.)	*Plural* (= acc.)
iste > este	istos > estos
ista > esta	istas > estas
ipse > ese	ipsos > esos
ipsa > esa	ipsas > esas
istud > esto	
ipsud > eso	

The etymology of *aquel, -la, -los, -las* has been suggested as *eccu ille*. (*Ecce* [meaning *he aquí* in Spanish] was used in Classical Latin preceding demonstratives for emphasis, and its linguistic descendants are current in a number of modern French and Italian forms.) Arriving at the stage *equel*, the initial *e* could have dissimilated to *a*. *Atque ille* has also been postulated, and makes *aquel* easier to derive phonetically, but semantically (*atque* = 'and even') it is weak.

Relatives and Interrogatives

§163. From the Vulgar Latin relative and interrogative pronoun declension, the only members to survive were the nominative singular *qui*, the accusative singular *quem*, and the neuter singular *quid*. The first two developed to *qui* and *quién* in Spanish, and *both* were used interchangeably in Old Spanish as singulars *or* plurals, nominatives *or* accusatives. In the 14th century, however, *qui* fell into disuse. During the 16th century, an analogical plural was created for *quién: quiénes*.
The neuter *quid* developed into the interrogative *¿qué?* and the

unstressed *quem* also became *que (la chica que veo)*; the two *que*'s working together were able to oust other related Latin words: *melius* quam > *mejor que, credo* quia > *creo que* (§74c).

Other interrogatives developed without complication:

de unde > ¿dónde? quando > ¿cuándo?
quale > ¿cuál? quomodo > ¿cómo?

Positive and Negative Words

§164. A number of Classical Latin positive and negative words were dropped and new ones formed in Vulgar Latin. The past participle *natus* 'born' used in a negative sense gave rise to two of the new formations in Hispania: *(res) nata* '([no]thing) born' replaced CL *nihil* 'nothing'. CL *nemo* was replaced by a form of *(hominem) natum* '([no] man) born' = 'no one'. CL *etiam* was replaced by *tam bene*.

aliqu'unu > alguno   (res) nata > nada
aliquod > algo   semper > siempre
iam > ya   tam bene > también
numquam > nunca   tota via > todavía

To complete this list, there are three words which require some explanation: *alguien, ninguno* and *nadie*.

CL *áliquem* would have yielded *algue* in Spanish, but it changed its stress based on the model of the stressed monosyllable *quem*(Sp. *quién*), giving *alguién*. To make its stress uniform with *algo* (and other positive and negative words), the stress then moved back to its original place: *álguien*.

Nec + unu is the basis for *ningun(o)*. *Necunu* would develop normally to *neguno*, but two things happened to it. First, an *n* appeared that made the form *nenguno* in Old Spanish. This *n* could be analogical with the *n* of *bien, sin, con, en*, but it also seems plausible that the initial *n* might have nasalized the entire syllable, causing another *n* to be created before the *g*, much like the Portuguese *muito*, which is pronounced with an *n* preceding the *t*: [mwĩntu]. The second feature, the appearance of *i* in the first syllable, is analogical with *ni*.

The process by which *natu* changed into *nadie* is not usually explained convincingly. Traditionally, *nado +* the *i* of *qui* is said to have been given OSp. *nadi*, and *nado +* the final *e* of *este, ese* was supposed to have given OSp. (rare) *nade*. A merging of the two *was supposed to have given* **nadie**. It could be, however, that *nadi* was influenced by its positive form, *alguien*, to give *nadien*, which lost its final *n* early by dissimilation with the initial *n* (§149c). (In modern times a *new* dialectical *nadien* has been created again, analogical with *alguien*.)

Possessives

§165. The possessives developed into two distinct sets in modern Spanish: a *stressed* set where the possessive is a stressed word and follows the noun (*este amigo* mío), and an unstressed set where the possessive precedes the noun as a proclitic (mi *amigo*). Whereas the two sets are differentiated in modern Spanish in all forms except *nuestro* and *vuestro*, they were quite close in form in Old Spanish as the developments below show. It could be even postulated that the forms of the 'unstressed' set were actually stressed in Old Spanish since the 'unstressed' VL *meu*, *nostru* and *vostru* show *stressed* vowel development in Old Spanish.

Whereas Classical Latin possessives had the same vowel quality in both the masculine and feminine forms of the singular (*mĕum, mĕam; tŭum, tŭam; sŭum, sŭam*), in Vulgar Latin, the feminine form showed a close vowel (*mẹu, mẹa; tụu, tụa; sụu, sụa*);[3] this feature affected both sets of possessives.

a. The stressed possessives developed in this way from Vulgar Latin to Old Spanish:

mẹu > mieo (§81b*i*) > OSp. mío	mẹos > mieos > OSp. míos
mẹa > OSp. mía	mẹas > OSp. mías
tụu > OSp. to	tụos > tos
tụa > OSp. tua	tụas > OSp. tuas
sụu > OSp. so	sụos > OSp. sos
sụa > OSp. sua	sụas > OSp. suas
nọstru > OSp. nuestro	nọstros > OSp. nuestros
nọstra > OSp. nuestra	nọstras > OSp. nuestras
vọstru > OSp. vuestro	vọstros > OSp. vuestros
vọstra > OSp. vuestra	vọstras > OSp. vuestras

In Old Spanish, *mío* existed along with *mió*, the latter being actually a normal development, parallel to that of *Deus*, which gave *Diéos, Díos,* and finally *Diós.*

---

[3] §78 gives one attested example where the *e* of *mea* actually rose to *i*, yielding VL *via*.

⌄

The feminine form of the possessives was dominant; based on the forms *tua(s)* and *sua(s)*, the Old Spanish *to(s)* and *so(s)* became *tuo(s)* and *suo(s)*. These latter forms are rarely seen in the old language because of another analogy which quickly affected all of the forms. *Tuyo(s)* and *suyo(s)* were created by analogy based either on *cuyo* or the *i* of *mío*. Already in the *Poema del Cid, tuyo* and *suyo* are commonly seen.

b. In Vulgar Latin, some of the unstressed possessives began to appear in shortened form due to proclitic use; they developed into Old Spanish in this way:

męu > OSp. mío	męos > OSp. míos
męa > OSp. míe, mi	męas > OSp. míes, mis
tụ > OSp. to	tụs > OSp. tos
tụa > OSp. túe, tu	tụas > OSp. túes, tus
sụ > OSp. so	sụs > OSp. sos
sụa > OSp. súe, su	sụas > OSp. súes, sus
nǫstru > OSp. nuestro	nǫstros > OSp. nuestros
nǫstra > OSp. nuestra	nǫstras > OSp. nuestras
vǫstru > OSp. vuestro	vǫstros > OSp. vuestros
vǫstra > OSp. vuestra	vǫstras > OSp. vuestras

The final *e* of *míe(s)* is said to be due to an assimilation of the *-a*, approaching the point of articulation of the *i*. The final *e* of *túe(s)* and *súe(s)* would then be analogical with *míe(s)*. Here again, the masculine forms conformed to feminine development and became *mi(s), tu(s)* and *su(s)* in modern Spanish.

Nuestro and *vuestro*, which had no hiatus problem to complicate their development, evolved the same way in both sets of possessives.

Numbers

§166. The cardinal numbers offer few problems in their development from Vulgar Latin to Spanish. The numbers *unu, duos* and *tres* were declinable in Vulgar Latin (§45a), but in Spanish only *uno* differentiates between masculine and feminine.

a. The development of 1 - 10 from Vulgar Latin to Spanish is as follows:

unu, -a > uno, -a	sex > seis
duos > dos	sette > siete
tres > tres	octo > ocho
quatt(u)or > cuatro	nove > nueve
cinque > cinco	dece > diez

The phonology of *cuatro* and *seis* is explained in §148a. The final *o* of *cinco* is analogical with the -*o* of *cuatro*.

b. The development of 11 - 19 is as follows:

und(e)ce > once		dece et sex > dieciséis	
dodece > doce		dece et sette > diecisiete	
tred(e)ce > trece		dece et octo > dieciocho	
catordece > catorce		dece et nove > diecinueve	
quind(e)ce > quince			

Normal phonetic development would have caused *dod(e)ce* and *tredece* to become *doz* and *trez* (§95a), but analogy with *once* (where the *e* could not fall since the *c* began the last syllable, and there would be *no* syllable possible without the *e*), and also the need to keep the forms fully divorced phonetically from *dos* and *tres*, caused the *e* not to drop. CL *quattuordecim* must have lost its initial wau by dissimilation (as in CL *quinque* > VL *cinque*), and then the second wau was dropped as was normal before all vowels but *a*.

c. The tens showed this development from Vulgar Latin:

viínte > veínte > véinte	sexaénta > sesenta
tríinta > treínta > tréinta	settaénta > setenta
quadraénta > cuarenta	octoénta > ochenta
cinquaénta > cincuenta	novaénta > noventa

Veinte and *treinta* need some explanation. The final long *i* of CL *vīgĭntī*, in accordance with §110, raised the stressed short *i* (which normally would have developed to *e*) to *i*. The final eventually *i* became *e* itself, and the result was *viínte*. There was then a dissimilation of the two *i*'s (as in CL *vīcīnum* > Sp. *vecino*, §149d). From there, the stress shifted to the more open vowel to give *veínte*. Since CL *trīgĭnta* does not end in a long *i*, it should have given Sp. *trienta*; but it modeled itself after *veinte*, and the result was *treinta*.

d. The plural hundreds derive from the accusative plural (with final *os* and *as*) and therefore distinguish between masculine and feminine genders. *Ciento* has inherited its invariable nature from Classical Latin.

centu > ciento, cien
ducentos > OSp. dozientos > Sp. doscientos
trecentos > OSp. trezientos > Sp. trescientos
quadragintos (not continued)
quingentos > quinientos

sexcentos > seiscientos
septengentos (not continued)
octingentos (not continued)
nongentos (not continued)

Cien is a carryover from Old Spanish apocopated *cient* (as modern *gran* is a continuation of OSp. *grant.*) APOCOPATION is merely the loss of a final vowel.

Analogy with *dos* and *tres* caused *dozientos* and *trezientos* to change to *doscientos* and *trescientos. Quinientos* and *seiscientos* reflect normal development (although *quiñentos* would be a more traditional spelling for the former.)

The remaining forms (*cuatrocientos, setecientos, ochocientos, novecientos*) are analogical with the basic number to which was added *-cientos*. It should be noted how *sete-* and *nove-* properly show pretonic vowel development.

e. In the thousands, *mille* gave *mil* in accordance with §133b. The Latin system of using the neuter plural for multiples of thousands (*due milia, tria milia,* §45d) was naturally lost. Instead, Old Spanish expressed them this way: *dos vezes mil, tres vezes mil.* Modern Spanish has eliminated the word *veces: dos mil, tres mil. Millón* was an Italian 'invention' (It. *milione*) which Spanish borrowed during the Middle Ages.

§167. The ordinal number system in Spanish shows learned forms exclusively starting with sexto. CL *primus* and *tertius* were replaced by VL *primariu* and *tertiariu.*

primariu > primero	sextu (learned sexto)
secundu > segundo	septimu (learned séptimo)
tertiariu > tercero	octavu (learned octavo)
quarto > cuarto	nonu (learned noveno)
quintu > quinto	decimu (learned décimo)

The old language continued *septimu* as *sietmo, octavu* as *ochavo,* and *decimu* as *diezmo.* (*Ochavo* is retained in the language as the name of an old coin, and *diezmo* os continued in the meaning 'tithe'). *Noveno* is taken from the Latin distributive number system. (*Docena* and *decena* are other common examples reflecting the Latin distributive system.)

Personal Pronouns

§168a. The personal pronouns evolved from Vulgar Latin with some interesting developments. Here is how the nominative first and second person pronouns developed from Vulgar Latin to Spanish:

ego > ieo > yo
tu > tú
nos > OSp. nos (+ otros) > nosotros
vos > OSp. vos (+ otros) > vosotros

Eo became *yo* in accordance with §41a; *nos* and *vos* had emphatic collateral forms in Vulgar Latin, *nos alteros* and *vos alteros,* and it was these forms that finally ousted *nos* and *vos* at the end of the Middle Ages in Spain.

Usted comes from an eroded development of *vuestra merced* through shortened forms such as *vuasted* and *vusted. Ustedes* is an analogical plural built on *usted.*

b. In Vulgar Latin, the first and second person object pronouns developing from the Classical Latin dative case (Sp. *mí, ti, nos, os*) became the *stressed* direct *or* indirect object pronouns, and the pronouns that came from the Classical Latin accusative case (Sp. *me, te, nos, os*) became the *unstressed* direct *or* indirect object pronouns (§41b). Spanish has maintained this distinction everywhere except in the plural of the stressed set where subject pronouns have been substituted:

Stressed (= dat.)	*Unstressed* (= acc.)
mi > mí	me > me
ti > ti	te > te
nos > (nosotros)	nos > nos
vos > (vosotrtos)	vos > os

Os is said to have developed due to the phonetic conflict caused in commands. The *-dv-* of *venidvos* (and all other such commands) proved to be too much phonetically, so the *v* dropped: OSp. *venidos.*

c. The third person pronouns developed from the same Latin demonstratives which gave rise to the definite articles (§158a), but with certain variations. The Vulgar Latin distinctions between the dative and accusative pronouns remains in the Spanish unstressed pronouns, unlike those of the preceding section:

Nominative (Subject Pronouns)—Stressed

il(le) > él   illos > ellos
illa > ella   illas > ellas
illud > ello

Dative (Indirect Object Pronouns)—Unstressed

(il)li > le   (il)lis > les

Accusative (Direct Object Pronouns)—Unstressed

(il)lu > lo   (il)los > los
(il)la > la   (il)las > las

The dative and accusative pronouns lost a syllable due to their proclitic nature, but the nominative pronouns (excepting *él*) did not lose a syllable since they were the stressed set. *Il(le)* apparently lost the final *e* due to the tendency of final *e* to drop (§§95, 133b).

Since CL *illī, illīs*, with long final *i*, gave VL *(il)li, (il)lis*, the forms *li* and *lis* might be expected in Spanish, but because these pronouns were used proclitically, the *i* was treated as unstressed, and the modern forms are thus *le* and *les*.

Because *all* of the forms of the dative and accusative were used for *unstressed* third person object pronouns (unlike the singular pronouns of *b* above), the *stressed* object pronouns were taken from the only remaining source, the subject pronouns. A fortunate outcome from using the subject pronouns here is that they allow distinctions that would otherwise be impossible: *lo veo a* él; *lo veo a* usted.

d. The problem of *se lo* (= *le lo*) puzzles every generation of learners of Spanish. The historical development will explain this seemingly anamolous structure.

When two Classical Latin pronouns were grouped together, the dative preceded the accusative: CL *illī illum, illī illās*. As these two pronouns developed, the first one lost its initial vowel as it did when it stood alone. But since the two pronouns were virtually fused together, the 'initial' *i* of the second pronoun was not lost because it was really no longer in initial position. The development of the examples at this point in Vulgar Latin could be imagined as *lielo, lielas*. As these evolved into Old Spanish, the initial *l* + yod developed to [ʒ] (as the same cluster did in *muliere* > OSp. *muger* [muʒ'ar]. The above sets in Old Spanish looked like this: *gelo, gelas* [ǯélo, ǯélas]. In accordance with §141, [ǯ] evolved to [š], which is quite close to the [s] sound. The change from [šélo, šélas] to [sélo, sélas] was easily made, especially since there was a good analogy with the reflexive *se*, which appeared in similar syntactic patterns: *gelo dio (a él), se lo dio (a sí mismo)*. The plural form, which was seen in a few Old Spanish examples in variants of *leslo* (a normal development since there was no Vulgar Latin yod, as there was in the singular), soon was overpowered by the singular form, and in modern Spanish *se lo* represents both *le + lo* and *les + lo*.

    e. *Mecum, tecum* and *secum* (§41a, note) developed to *micum, ticum* and *sicum* in the Vulgar Latin of Hispania, corresponding to the stressed object pronouns of *b* above. These developed phonetically in the normal way to give *migo, tigo* and *sigo*. Since *cum* had been so transformed (into *go*) and looked nothing like *con* (which was the usual phonetic outcome of *cum* when standing alone, §147b), the preposition *con* was prefixed to *migo, tigo* and *sigo* to yield the modern forms *conmigo, contigo* and *consigo*; thus CL *cum* is represented *twice* in the modern Spanish forms.

The Development of Verbs

Infinitives

    §169. The Spanish language inherited almost all Vulgar Latin infinitives with only a few complications.

    a. The Vulgar Latin *-are* infinitives passed into Spanish smoothly. Among the examples below, *fabulare* was deponent in Classical Latin (§62):

circare > cercar	lucrare > lograr
clamare > llamar	mesurare > mesurar
coll(o)care > colgar	mutare > mudar
fab(u)lare > hablar	nom(i)nare > nombrar
lavare > lavar	plicare > llegar

The *-ar* verbs are the most common and the most regular in the language, and virtually every new verb that has come into the language, be it based on an adjective, a noun, or a newly created word, is an *-ar* verb: *fechar, fotografear, fusilar, mejorar, igualar, ocasionar, telefonear*.

    Andar is a very mysterious infinitive; its origin has never been identified with certainty, although there are a number of theories about it. The least likely conjecture is the one that derives *andar* (through metathesis) from *adnare* 'to swim to'. More reasonable is the theory that says that the noun *ambitus* 'detour' gave rise to an infinitive *ambitare* which would then give *andar* through normal phonetic evolution (*ambitare* > *ambidare* > *ambdar* > *andar*). Semantically, the best choice is *ambulare* 'to walk', but this form would have developed to *amblar*. If there had been a change of suffix in Vulgar Latin which had made *ambulare* into *ambutare*, then *andar* would be the normal development.

b. The Vulgar Latin -*ere* infinitives usually passed into Spanish without difficulty. The sampling below includes examples from the Classical Latin second conjugation (-*ēre*), as well as from the Classical third conjugation infinitives (CL *bíbĕre, cumédĕre, fácĕre, légĕre, pónĕre, sápĕre, véndĕre,* §51a), a few Vulgar Latin inchoatives that derived from non-inchoative Classical infinitives (CL *carēre, oboedīre, parēre,* §49b), and the Vulgar Latin infinitive *potére,* which replaced the irregular CL *posse* (§63):

> bibére (CL *bíbĕre*) > beber
> carescére (CL *carēre*) > carecer
> comedére (CL *cumédĕre*) > comer
> debére > deber
> facére (CL *fácĕre*) > hacer
> jacére > yacer
> habére > haber
> legére (CL *légĕre*) > leer
> obedescere (CL *oboedīre*) > obedecer
> parescére (CL *parēre*) > parecer
> ponére (CL *pónĕre*) > poner
> potére (CL *pósse*) > poder
> sapére (CL *sápĕre*) > saber
> tenére (CL *ténĕre*) > tener
> timére (CL *tímĕre*) > temer
> vendére (CL *véndĕre*) > vender
> vidére > ver

The Vulgar Latin infinitive *éssere* (which replaced CL *esse*) was not continued into Spanish; Sp. *ser* derived from CL *sedēre.*

There are two remnants of the CL -*ēre* infinitives surprisingly left in Spanish. CL *fácĕre* and *dícĕre* had a double development; the first one was their conjugation group change to OSp. *fazer* and *dizer,* but there was another development which maintained the Classical Latin stress.

fácere > fácre > fáre > OSp. far > Sp. har
dícere > dícre > díre > dir

These alternate infinitives are seen exclusively in the formation of
the future and conditional tenses in Spanish: *haré, diría*.

c. Vulgar Latin *-ire* infintives also transferred to Spanish intact.
The sampling below includes those infinitives that Vulgar Latin
inherited from the CL *i̯* third conjugation (*fúgiō, -ĕre; páriō, -ĕre;*
recípiō, -ĕre, §51b), those that derive from the Classical second conjugation (CL *implēre, lucēre, ridēre*, §51c), and VL *sequire*, which
was deponent in Classical Latin (*sequī*, §62):

audíre > oír
dormíre > dormir
fugire (CL *fúgĕre*) > huir
glattíre > latir
implíre (CL *implēre*) > henchir
lucíre (CL *lucēre*) > lucir
paríre CL *parĕre*) > parir
partíre > partir
recipíre (CL *recípĕre*) > recibir
ridíre (CL *ridēre*) > reír
sentíre > sentir
sequíre (CL *séquī*) > seguir
servíre > servir
veníre > venir

There were other Classical Latin third conjugation infinitives which
joined the above. The *-gĕre* infinitives switched to *-ir* in Spanish for
reasons that are not clear: CL *cíngĕre* > Sp. *ceñir*, CL *ríngĕre* > Sp.
reñir, CL *spárgĕre* > Sp. *esparcir*. Those *-ĕre* infinitives with *i* in the
stem also became *-ir* verbs in Spanish, sometimes with vocalic dissimilation (§149d), as in the first two of the following examples:
CL *dícĕre* > VL *dicire* > Sp. *decir*, CL *frígĕre* > VL *frigire* > Sp.
freír, CL *scríbĕre* > Sp. *escribir*, CL *vívĕre* > Sp. *vivir*. Classical Latin
pétĕre had a double set of perfects, one based on the *-ire* verbs
(*petīvī*) and the other based on the *-ĕre* verbs (*pétuī*). It was probably due to its *-ire* perfect that the rest of the conjugation also
switched to the *-ire* pattern: Sp. *pedir*.

The Present Indicative

§170. The present indicative, although it forms a fairly content system in modern Spanish, has quite a complicated history. In fact, it is precisely because the language strove to regularize the conjugations and maintain a constant stem throughout the present indicative that most of the historical complications have come about. The pressure to regularize the conjugations was so great that normal phonetic evolution was actually stunted in many cases. Indeed, whereas phonetic 'laws' are quite strong in themselves, morphological 'laws' are even stronger and of more consequence, as the sections below will explain.

For the time being, model conjugations will be given which show no complications after the Vulgar Latin stage. Where the Vulgar Latin form differs significantly from the Classical form, the latter will be given in parentheses. In §50 there are examples of complete Classical Latin present indicative conjugations.

§171a. This is the normal development of the present indicative from Vulgar Latin to Spanish of the verbs deriving from the Classical Latin first conjugation, -āre:

> clámo > llamo
> clámas > llamas
> clámat > llama
> clamámus > llamamos
> clamátis > OSp. llamades > Sp. llamáis
> clámant > llaman

The only unusual feature found above concerns the -atis > -áis development. In the fifteenth century, the -d- of -ades disappeared, and thw -e- *changed to yod. Ordinarily, the -d-* deriving from -t- was not lost in Spanish (§125a). The loss of -d- also affected the endings of the remaining conjugations (-etis > -éis, -itis > -ís).

b. Because there are many -are verbs which changed their tonic ŏ to ué or their ĕ *to ié,* a few verbs which showed an ō or an ē in Classical Latin have diphthongized by analogy, especially those verbs in which -ns follows the vowel in question:

> CL cōlat > Sp. cuela
> CL cōnstat > Sp. cuesta
> CL mōnstrat > Sp. muestra
> CL pēnsat > Sp. piensa
> CL rĭcat > Sp. riega
> CL sēminat > Sp. siembra

On the other hand, some verbs which should have diphthongized show a simple vowel in modern Spanish:

CL confōrta > Sp. conforta
CL vĕtat > Sp. veda

A few verbs which did have diphthongs in Old Spanish have lost them in modern Spanish since the diphthongs follow *muta cum liquida* (§81c): CL *intĕgrat* > OSp. *entriega* > Sp. *entrega*, CL *praestō* > OSp. *priesto* > Sp. *presto*

c. The Classical Latin verb *lĕvāre* presents an interesting development. In Old Spanish it developed to *levar* and was conjugated *lievo, lievas, lieva, levamos, levades, lievan*. It is easy to see that the four forms with *li-* became confused with *ll-*, and finally the whole conjugation, including the infinitive as well as the *nosotros* and *vosotros* forms, changed to the *ll-* pronunciation and spelling.

d. The Classical Latin verb *jŏcāre* presents a real phonetic problem in the modern Spanish *jugar*. It has been suggested that the verb could have deriverd from VL *jugare*, but in that case, the Old Spanish result would have had no diphthongized forms (which it did have in fact: OSp. *juego, juegas, juega, juegan*). It has also been suggested that *jugar* represents a Leonese development where the diphthong *ué* has generalized into the infinitive, then simplified to *u*; VL *jocare* would have given Leon. *juegar* and then simplified to *jugar*, as in VL Leon. > *cuentar* > Leon. *cuntar*. It does not seem likely, however, that such a common verb could come from a dialect.

§172. Here is the normal development of the present indicative from Vulgar Latin to Spanish of the verbs deriving from the Classical Latin second conjugation, *-ēre*:

débo (CL *debēo*) > debo
débes > debes
débet > debe
debémus > debemos
debétis > OSp. debedes > Sp. debéis
débent > deben

It was pointed out in §51c that in some verbs, the *-e-* of the Classical Latin first person singular was slow to drop and became a yod, the result being that these particular verbs moved to the *-ire* conjugation in Vulgar Latin. The *-e-* in the usual case, as in the model conjugation above, dropped without leaving a trace. Other examples of this include: CL *tǐmeō* > Sp. *temo*, CL *mǒveō* > Sp. *muevo*.

CL *vídeō* developed in the normal way to *veyo* in Old Spanish (§129a). The triphthong was then reduced by the removal of the middle element, and the modern *veo* came into existence. CL *vides*, *videt*, *vidēre* gave *vees*, *vẹe*, *veer* in Old Spanish. When the infinitive simplified to *ver*, the other forms based themselves on the new infintitives: *ves*, *ve*. This development contrasts with *lee* and *cree* in §173b, where the infinitive is based on the conjugated forms.

§173a. This is the normal development from Vulgar Latin to Spanish of the verbs deriving from the Classical Latin third conjugation, *-ěre*:

> bíbo > bebo
> bíbes (CL *bíbis*) > bebes
> bíbet (CL *bíbit*) > bebe
> bibémus (CL *bíbimus*) > bebemos
> bibétis (CL bíbitis) > OSp. bebedes > Sp. bebéis
> bíbent (CL Cbíbunt) > beben

In Vulgar Latin, the Classical Latin third conjugation merged with the Classical second conjugation (§51a); this included second conjugation verb endings as well as second conjugation stress (§52).

b. With the fall of intervocalic *d* and *g* (§§129a, 130a), one might expect CL *crēdit* to yield Sp. *crey* and *lēgit* to give *ley*, in accordance with §95a. However, due to the morphological pressure to maintain consistent verb endings, these two verbs did not give in to normal phonetic development, and became *cree* and *lee*.

§174. This is the normal development of the present indicative from Vulgar Latin to Spanish of the verbs from the Classical fourth conujugation, *-īre*:

> dórmo (CL *dórmiō*) > duermo
> dórmis > duermes
> dórmit > duerme
> dormímus > dormimos
> dormítis > OSp. dormides > Sp. dormís
> dórment (CL *dormiunt*) > duermen

The yod in the Classical Latin first person singular ending was usually lost in Vulgar Latin (§50), but in many instances, the yod was slower to disappear than it was in the model above, in which case it caused some phonetic and morphological difficulties, as will be explained in §176; Other examples which show early loss of the yod include: CL *apériō* > Sp. *abro*, CL *fēriō* > Sp. *hiero*, CL *partiō* > Sp. *parto*.

OSp. *-ides* would have given *-íes*, *-iés* with loss of *-d-*. But in this case, since *-ades* gave *-áis*, *-ides* followed suit yielding *-íis* which simplified to *-ís*. The Vulgar Latin third person plural ending is analogical with the *-ent* of the *-ere* conjugation (§172).

§175. A few additional comments should be made about the leveling of Classical Latin stress in Vulgar Latin. In Classical Latin, a verb would be stressed in some persons on the first syllable of the stem (*áperis*, *súccutis*), and in other persons on the second syllable of the stem (*apério*, *succútio*). This variance of stress evened out in Vulgar Latin, but not in a uniform way. Some verbs unified their stress based on the first person singular: VL *ápero*, *áperis*, *áperit*, and others unified their stress based on the pattern of the remaining forms: VL *sucúto*, *sucútis*, *sucútit*. This Vulgar Latin stress was maintained in Spanish: *ábro*, *ábres*, *ábre*; *sacúdo*, *sacúdes*, *sacúde*.

It should be also mentioned, since Spanish always stresses the present tense verbs on the penult (except for the *vosotros* form), that 'learned' verbs which have been added into the language do not maintain 'learned' stress, but change it to fit the normal Spanish pattern:

CL *cólloco* > Sp. *colóco*
CL *commúnico* > Sp. *comuníco*
CL *consídero* > Sp. *considéro*
CL *víndico* > Sp. *vindíco*

The first, second and fourth of these in their traditional developments, have maintained the original Latin stress:

CL *cóll(o)cō* > Sp. *cuélgo*
CL *commún(i)cō* > Sp. *comúlgo*
CL *vínd(i)cō* > Sp. *véngo*

§176a. The present tense of *-ir* verbs shows quite a bit of inflection and anology not seen in *-ar* and *-er* verbs. It was stated in §52 and again in §174 that the yod of the first person singular endings in some third and most fourth conjugation present indicatives in Vulgar Latin dropped without leaving a trace (CL *faciō* > VL *faco*

> Sp. *hago*, CL *partiō* > VL *parto* > Sp. *parto*). However, when the stem vowel of a Vulgar Latin -*ire* verb was a close *e* (deriving from CL *ē* or *i̯*), the VL yod raised it to *i* before it disappeared. This effect is seen universally in the earliest Castilian texts. Thus VL *me̜-tio* became *mido* already in Old Spanish. On the other hand, one would expect that VL *me̜tis*, *me̜tit* and *me̜tent* would yield *medes*, *mede* and *meden* in Spanish since no yod followed their close *e*. However, these forms do not exist in Spanish, and for a very good reason. In the -*ar* and -*er* cojugations, where there is a vowel change, it affects *all four* strong forms, as these examples show:

-AR		*-ER*	
s*ie*nto	sentamos	v*ue*lvo	volvemos
s*ie*ntas	sentáis	v*ue*lves	volvéis
s*ie*nta	s*ie*ntan	v*ue*lve	v*ue*lven

By analogy, the -*ir* verbs with an inflected first person singular followed the model of the -*ar* and -*er* verbs and placed an -*i*- in the remaining strong forms. Thus:

Vulgar Latin	*Spanish*
métio	m*i*do
métis	m*i*des
métit	m*i*de
me̜tímus	medimos
me̜títis	medís
métent	m*i*den

This analogical feature affecting the second and third persons singular and third person singular is again seen in the earliest Castilian texts.

This phenomenon also affected verbs with a yod which came to the VL -*ire* from other sources, as this sampling shows:

CL ĭmplēre,	VL ịmplēre > Sp. henchir
ĭmpleō	VL ịmplio > Sp. h*i*ncho
	VL ịmplis > Sp. h*i*nches (anal.)
	VL ịmplimus > Sp. henchimos
CL concĭpĕre,	VL concịpire > Sp. concebir
concĭpiō	VL concịpio > Sp. conc*i*bo
	VL concịpis > Sp. conc*i*bes (anal.)
	VL concịpimus > Sp.concebimos

It should be pointed out that the Spanish result of CL *recĭpĕre*, practically a twin of *concĭpĕre*, has generalized the *i* everywhere whereas *coˀɪcĭpĕre* has not:

CL recĭpĕre,   VL recĭpire > Sp. recíbir (anal.)
VL recīpiō   VL recĭpio > Sp. recíbo
               VL recĭpis > Sp. recíbes (anal.)
               VL recĭpimus > Sp.recíbimos (anal.)

b. The above deals with *-ir* verbs with a Classical Latin close *e* as their stem vowel. But what about those *-ir* verbs which had an open *e*?

One could expect, on pure phonetic grounds, that the Vulgar Latin yod would raise the open *e* to a close *e* in the first person singular only, but that the remaining three strong forms, lacking a yod in their endings, would be free to show a diphthonigized vowel, thus, these conjugations (which do *not* exist exactly as listed below) could have been expected:

Vulgar Latin	Spanish	Vulgar Latin	Spanish
sérvio	servo	séntio	sento
sérvis	sierves	séntis	sientes
sérvit	sierve	séntit	siente
servímus	servimos	sentímus	sentimos
servítis	servís	sentítis	sentís
sérvent	sierven	séntent	sienten

Since neither *servir* nor *sentir* is conjugated as phonetically predicted, how can the existing Spanish conjugations of these two verbs be explained? Again, it is analogy at work, and each example shows a different type of analogy. *Servir* has merely modeled itself after the *medir* type, using this ratio formula: *medimos : servimos :: mido : x* (=sirvo). Once *sirvo* was formed, *sirves, sirve, sirven* followed suit, as explained in *a* above. Other verbs that work like *servir* are *vestir*, from CL *vĕstīre* (Sp. *visto*, not *vesto*), and *embestir* from CL *ĭnvĕstīre* (Sp. *embisto*, not *embesto*).

The more common case is what happened with *sentir*. Here, the first person singular simply yielded to the morphological pressure exerted by the other strong forms and took an analogical *-ie-*. Other verbs that work like *sentir* include *herir*, from CL *fĕrīre* (Sp. *hiero*, not *hero*) and *mentir*, from CL *mentīre* (Sp. *miento*, not *mento*).

c. A number of Classical Latin verbs which had no first person singular yod joined the Vulgar Latin -*ire* conjugation, and many of these, by analogy, followed the 'inflected' conjugation described above in *a*. The Classical Latin infinitives and first person singulars are given for better comparison:

Classical Latin	Spanish
cĭngĕre, cĭngō	ceñir, c*i*ño
dīcĕre, dīcī,	decir, d*i*go
pĕtĕre, pĕtō	pedir, p*i*do
rĕgĕre, rĕgō	regir, r*i*jo
sĕquī, sĕquor	seguir, s*i*go

d. The other type of -*ire* conjugation inflection was where close *o* was raised to *u* in the Old Spanish first person singular. In these verbs, the first person was so powerful that *all* forms of the verb, every person of every tense, not just the strong forms of the present (as in *a* above), eventually took the *u* as their theme vowel. In the examples below, from CL *sŭbīre* and *coŏpĕrīre*, the modern Spanish forms reveal analogical generalization of the *u*:

Vulgar Latin	Old Spanish	Spanish
sŭbire	sobir	s*u*bir (*anal.*)
sŭbio	s*u*bo	s*u*bo
sŭbis	sobes	s*u*bes (*anal.*)
sŭbit	sobe	s*u*be (*anal.*)
sŭbimus	sobimos	s*u*bimos (*anal.*)
sŭbitis	sobides	s*u*bís (*anal.*)
sŭbent	soben	s*u*ben (*anal.*)
cŏp(e)rire	cobrir	c*u*brir (*anal.*)
cŏp(e)rio	c*u*bro	c*u*bro
cŏp(e)ris	cobres	c*u*bres (*anal.*)
cŏp(e)rit	cobre	c*u*bre (*anal.*)
cŏp(e)rimus	cobrimos	c*u*brimos (*anal.*)
cŏp(e)ritis	cobrides	c*u*brís (*anal.*)
cŏp(e)rent	cobren	c*u*bren (*anal.*)

This phenomenon affected verbs with a yod that joined the Vulgar Latin -*ire* conjugation from other Classical Latin sources, as this sampling shows:

CL cōmplēre,   VL complire > OSp. complir > Sp. cumplir (*anal.*)
    cōmpleō   VL complio > OSp. cumplo > Sp. cumplo
               VL complis > OSp. comples > Sp. cumples (*anal.*)
               VL complimus > OSp. complimos > Sp. cumples (*anal.*)

CL fūgĕre,   VL fugire > OSp. foír > Sp. huír (*anal.*)
    fūgiō   VL fugio > OSp. fuyo > Sp. huyo
               VL fugis > OSp. foes > Sp. huyes (*anal.*)
               VL fugimus > OSp. foímos > Sp.huímos (*anal.*)

CL sŭffere,   VL sufferire > OSp. sofrir > Sp. sufrir (*anal.*)
    sŭfferō   VL sufferio > OSp. sufro > Sp. sufro
               VL sufferis > OSp. sofres > Sp. sufres (*anal.*)
               VL sufferimus > OSp. sofrimos > Sp. sufrimos (*anal.*)

CL *sŭfferre* was a compound of the irregular *ferō (ferre)*, and it changed to the *-ire* conjugation in Vulgar Latin (§63).

e. In the case of VL *dormio* and *morio* (CL *morior*, a deponent verb), we could have expected the yod to raise the open *o* to a close *o* in Spanish giving these hypothetical forms: *dormo* and *moro*. The Spanish *duermo* and *muero* are quite obviously analogical forms based on the remaining strong forms with *ué*. This process is similar to the one described in section *b* above (with *siento*).

§177. In a number of first person singular forms in Spanish, a g has appeared where there seemingly is no reason for its being there. These forms fall into two different groups: 1) *caigo, oigo, traigo,* and 2) *vengo, pongo, tengo, salgo, valgo.*

a. The outcome of VL *cadeo* (CL *cadō*) and *audio* was *cayo* and *oyo* in Old Spanish; *traho* resulted in *trayo* through the addition of *y* to avoid hiatus.[4] The common and important Old Spanish verbs *digo* and *fago*, whose g is etymological, deriving from VL *dico* and *faco* (CL *faciō*), imposed a non-etymological g into *cayo, oyo* and *trayo*, causing them to become *caigo, oigo* and *traigo.*

b. The second set requires a different explanation as to why the g appeared when there was no apparent etymological reason. Certainly the Latin forms below could not directly result in the Spanish forms with g:

> VL tenio (CL *tĕneō*)—Sp. tengo
> VL valio (CL*valeō*)—Sp. valgo
> VL ponio (CL *pōnō*)—Sp. pongo
> VL salio—Sp. salgo
> VL venio—Sp. vengo

[4] Philologists call this spontaneously generated type of vowel an EPEN-THETIC vowel.

In the above Vulgar Latin forms, the yod could not have its effect in either of the two ways usually open to it. First, its action was thwarted because morphological pressure prevented it from mixing with the previous consonant, which would thus have impaired the consonantal unity of the stem of the verb (§176), and would have caused the first person singular forms to develop into these non existent examples: *teño, poño, sajo, veño* (although in Portuguese *tenho, ponho* and *venho* are indeed the normal results). The yod was again thwarted since in four of the five verbs it could not release its energy by inflecting the preceding vowel; only -*ire* verbs with an *e* or *o* as their stem vowel would allow inflection, and of the five verbs, only *venio* met these requirements. (In *venio* the open *e* was raised by the yod to a close *e*, thus there is no diphthong in the form.) Three of the other verbs are from the -*ere* conjugation, and the remaining verb, although from the -*ire* group, has *a* as its theme vowel, thus none of the remaining four was susceptible to inflection. Since the yod's energy *had* to be released, it was forced to find a third way—a new way—to expend itself. Since a *g* can become a yod (§§139,172b, 142a), it is plausible that a yod that is seeking a new outlet for its energy can become a *g*, especially since there was a nice analogy in Old Spanish of verbs which presented an etymological *g* in similar phonetic surroundings: *frango* (VL *frango*), *plango* (VL *plango*), *tango* (VL *tango*). Thus, the *g* in the five Spanish verbs above appears to derive from a yod.

§178. Another set of 'aggressive' first person singular forms were OSp. *oyo* and *fuyo*, whose *y* developed regularly from VL *audio* and *fugio*. This *y* was powerful in two ways. First, it propagated itself to the remaining strong forms of the present: *oyes, oye, oyen; fuyes, fuye, fuyen*. (The Vulgar Latin forms could not give rise to a *y* by themselves: *audis, audit, audent; fugis, fugit, fugent*.) Second, the *y* infiltrated into the strong forms of learned verbs such as *construir*, none of whose forms, not even the first person singular, had an etymological right to a *y*:

> CL cónstruo—Sp. construyo
> CL cónstruis—Sp. construyes
> CL cónstruit—Sp. construye
> CL cónstruunt—Sp. construyen

Among other verbs that follow this pattern are *argüir, atribuir, contribuir, destruir, diluir, disminuir, influir, sustitutir*.

§179. The modern verb forms *doy, soy, voy, estoy,* which have a final *y,* developed to their normal phonetic result in Old Spanish without *y*:

> VL dao (CL *dō*) > OSp. do
> VL sum > OSp. so[5]
> VL vao (CL *vadō*) > OSp. vo
> VL stao (CL *stō*)> OSp. estó

The earliest documentation of any of these four forms with final *y* is *doy* and dates from the early thirteenth century; the final *y* refers to the indirect object, as some of the examples below show. This Spanish *y* is similar to the French adverbial *y* of *j'y vais*:

> *do y* la otra heredat a este monasterio (Staaff, p. 39)
> *do.hy.* cuanto eredamiento a Sancta Maria de Piasca (Staaff, p. 39)
> *do.y.* ueinte uaccas (Staaff, p. 77)
> *do i* por mi alma . . . vi tabladas (*Doc. ling.,* p. 124)
> *do hi* conmigo quanto he (*Doc. ling.,* p. 134)[6]

It was not until the sixteenth century that the *-y* became permanently attached to the *do* and spread to *so* and *vo,* both of which were related to *do* since all three were common monosylabic first person singulars. (The *u* of *estoy* is analogical with *soy.*)

During this same period, *ha* 'there is, there are' also took a final *y,* which made it similar to the French construction il y a (Fr. y + *a* = Sp. *ha* + *y*).

§180a. The present tense of the verb *ser* developed from the Classical Latin *esse* conjugation with some modification:

> CL sum > OSp. so > Sp. soy (§179)
> CL es (*not continued*); eris > Sp. eres
> CL est > Sp. es
> CL sumus > Sp. somos
> CL estis (not continued); VL sutis > OSp. sodes > Sp. sois
> CL sunt > Sp. son

---

[5] *Son* would be the expected result from *sum,* as *tam* > *tan, quem* > *quien* (§147b), but *-n* was dropped in order to differentiate *so* from the third person plural *son* (< *sunt*).

[6] Staaff, Erik, *Étude sur l'ancien dialecte léonais (d'après des chartes du XIIIe. siècle),* Uppsala: Almqvist & Wiksell, 1907; Menéndez Pidal, Ramón, *Documentos lingüísticos de España (Vol. I, Reino de Castilla),* Madrid: Centro de estudios históricos, 1919.

Both CL *es and est* would have developed to *es* in Spanish; to avoid this confusion, the language retained the Classical Latin future (of *esse*) *eris* 'you will be', which developed to *eres*. This lone form is the only vestige of the Classical Latin future tense in Spanish, indeed, the only vestige of the Classical future in any of the major Romance Languages. CL *estis* was lost in Spanish, probably because its root was based on the *singular es, est*, and not on the plural forms; a new formation, *sutis*, based on *sumus, sunt*, was created, which gave *sois* in Spanish through normal phonetic evolution.

b. The Classical Latin infinitive *īre* was continued (Sp. *ir*), but none of its present tense conjugation has survived to modern Spanish; most of its forms would have been too short or too confusing: CL *ego eō* would have developed to to Sp. *yo yo*, for example. *Imos* (from CL *īmus*) and *ides* (from CL *ītis*) were the only forms of *īre* that were retained in Old Spanish.

It was the present indicative of CL *vadĕre* 'to walk' which replaced the present indicative of *īre* in Spanish:

CL vadō > VL vao > OSp. vo > Sp. voy (§179)
CL vadis > VL vas > Sp. vas
CL vadit > VL vat > Sp. va
CL vádimus > VL vamus > Sp. vamos
CL váditis > VL vatis > Sp. vais
CL vadunt > VL vant > Sp. van

§181. The conjugation of CL *habēre* lost a syllable in the Vulgar Latin strong forms (§54b):

CL habeo > VL aio > Sp. he
CL habes > VL as > Sp. has
CL habet > VL at > Sp. ha
CL habemus > VL abemus > OSp. (av)emos > Sp. hemos
CL habētis > VL abetis > Sp. habéis
CL habent > VL and > Sp. han

Restoration of the *h-* in Spanish is purely learned.

The development of the first person singular is obscure. The final *o* of the Vulgar Latin form had to be lost early for *ai* to become *ei* (as in Portuguese *hei*) then to simplify to *(h)e*. Compare *probai* > *probei* (as in Portuguese) > *probé* (§107). If the *o* had remained, *aio* would have given simply *hayo*, or possibly *haigo* by analogy with other verbs. The obscure point is, of course, why the *-o* fell inthe first place. In Old Spanish, *avemos* was regularly used for the main verb and for the auxiliary, whereas *emos* was seen used in connection with the formation of the future. It is this latter form which has survived in modern Spanish, both as an auxiliary (*lo* hemos *hecho*) and as the future ending (*lo* har*emos*).

§182. CL *sapére* has also given rise to a problem in the first person singular. *Sapio*, according to normal phonetic development pattern (§109), should have given *sepo*, as *sapiam* has given *sepa*. The usual explanation for *sé* is that is is analogical with *he*. This seems to be the most likely possibility since other Romance Languages have the same parallel in forms: It. *so, ho;* Port. *sei, hei;* Fr. *sais, ai* [sɛ, ɛ].

The Present Subjunctive

§183. The endings of the Classical Latin present subjunctive had the characteristics that the Spanish subjunctive was to retain: the *-are* conjugation had endings based on *e,* and the remaining conjugations had endings based on *a* (§65). Here are typical developments from Vulgar Latin to Spanish:

> *-are*
>
> clamem > llame
> clames > llame
> clamet > llame
> clamemus > llamemos
> clametis > llaméis
> clament > llamen
>
>   *-ere* (from CL *-ēre*)
>
> timam (CL *timeam*) > tema
> timas (CL *timeās*) > temas
> timat (CL *timeat*) > tema
> timamus (CL *timeāmus*) > temamos
> timatis (CL *timeātis*) > temáis
> timant (CL *timeant*) > teman
>
>   *-ere* (from CL *-ĕre*)
>
> bibam > beba
> bibas > bebas
> bibat > beba
> bibamus > bebamos
> bibatis > bebáis
> bibant > beban

-ire

partam (CL *partiam*) > parta
partas (CL *partiās*) > partas
partat (CL *partiat*) > partamos
partiamus (CL *partiāmus*) > partamos
partiatis (CL *partiātis*) > partáis
partant (CL *partiant*) > partan

The stem of the subjunctive was influenced by the stem of the indicative, and specifically by the first person singular. If *pacare* and *plicare*, for example, had developed according to phonetic convention, *pacem* would have given *pace* in Spanish, and *plicem* would have given *llece* (instead of *pague* and *llegue*), as noted in §126c, but the morphological pressure from the indicative prevented this normal phonetic change from taking place.

The yod which was lost in the first person singular of the present indicative of the Classical Latin *-ēre* conjugation (CL *timeo* > VL *timo*) was equally lost in the subjunctive in Vulgar Latin.

Those Spanish verbs which have a *g* in the first person singular of the indicative, whether it is etymological or not, have a *g* in all of the present subjunctive forms. In these same verbs, if there was no diphthongization in the first person singular of the present indicative (as in *tengo, vengo* below), there was no diphthongization in *any* form of the present subjunctive either. This again illustrates the immense influence of the first person singular of the present indicative.

CL dīcō > Sp. digo
CL dīcam > Sp. diga

CL tĕneō > Sp. tengo
CL tĕneat > Sp. tenga

CL vĕniō > Sp. vengo
CL vĕniās > Sp. vengas

§184a. In the *-ire* subjunctive conjugation, if the theme vowel was an *i, a* or *u*, the yod of the first and second person plural merely fell without leaving a trace, as in VL *partiamus* > Sp. *partamos* above.

b. If, however, the theme vowel of the *-ire* conjugation was an *e* or *o*, the yod of the first and second person plural raised them to *i* or *o*, then disappeared:

Vulgar Latin	Spanish
metiamus	midamos
metiatis	midáis
sentiamus	sintamos
sentitis	sintáis
dormiamus	durmamos
dormiatis	durmáis

Since Vulgar Latin initial vowels were close (§87), the yod only had to raise the *e* and *o* one step on the vowel triangle.

§185. A few words must be said about the irregular present subjunctives in Spanish, that is, the subjunctives that have a different stem from the first person singular present indicative.

a. The subjunctive of *esse* (CL *sim, sīs, sit, sīmus, sītis, sint*) would have developed into forms that were too short or too confusing in Spanish; the present subjunctive of CL *sedēre* replaced this conjugation:

VL sedeam > OSp. seya > Sp. sea
VL sedeas > OSp. seyas > Sp. seas
VL sedeat > OSp. seya > Sp. sea
VL sedeamus > OSp. seyamos > Sp. seamos
VL sedeatis > OSp. seyades > Sp. seáis
VL sedeant > OSp. seyan > Sp. sean

The Old Spanish stage, containing a triphthong beginning with *ey* dropped the yod as usual. Another example of this yod loss is seen in the development of *ver*: VL *videas* > OSp. *veyas* > Sp. *veas*.

b. The present subjunctive of *-ire* (CL *eam, eās, eat, eāmus, eātis, eant*) was equally lost, and for the same reasons as above. The subjunctive of *vadere* replaced it. In Old Spanish this subjunctive took an epenthetic *y* to remedy the unusual hiatus created by the loss of *d*, although one does occasionally see the etymological forms of the first and second persons plural in Old Spanish without *y: vaamos, vaades*.

vadam > vaya
vadas > vayas
vadat > vaya
vadamus > vayamos
vadatis > vayáis
vadant > vayan

The etymological result of *vadamus*, however, has survived as the positive *nosotros* imperative: *vamos*.

c. The present subjunctive of *habēre* shows the unusual loss of *b* before yod (§137b). The loss of *b* apparently ocurred in Vulgar Latin, similar to what happened in the indicative (§179):

> CL habeam > Sp. haya
> CL habeās > Sp. hayas
> CL habeat > Sp. haya
> CL habeāmus > Sp. hayamos
> CL habeātis > Sp. hayáis
> CL habeant > Sp. hayan

d. The present subjunctive of *dare* and *stāre* present a minor phonological problem. In all other *-are* subjunctives, the endings are unstressed (except for the first and second person plural), so it makes no difference that the first and third person singular and the third person plural have a CL *ĕ*, whereas the second person singular shows a CL *ē*; both *e*'s will result in *e* in Spanish (§93). However, in the case of *dare* and *stāre*, the endings contained the *stressed* vowels in these persons, so their first and third person singular and third person plural could have developed to *die*, *die*, *dien* and *estié*, *estié*, *estién*, but morphological pressure was too great to allow this seeming irregularity:

> CL dĕm > Sp. dé   CL stĕm > Sp. esté
> CL dēs > Sp. des   CL stēs > Sp. estés
> CL dĕt > Sp. dé   CL stĕs > Sp. esté
> CL dēmus > Sp. demos CL stēmus > Sp. estemos
> CL dētis > Sp. deis   CL stēmus > Sp. estemos
> CL dĕnt > Sp. den   CL stĕnt > Sp. estén

Imperatives

§186a. In Classical Latin, the imperatives existed only in the positive form, the negative form being expressed with the verb *noli(te)* 'be unwilling' + *infinitive* (§53). But Classical Latin also used the jussive subjunctive (*Frater meus id faciat!* 'Let my brother do it') as a type of imperative, both for the positive and for the negative. This subjunctive use laid the foundation for the Vulgar Latin *non* + *subjunctive* replacing the CL *noli(te)* + *infininitive* construction as the negative form of the imperative (§53).

The Spanish language continues the Classical Latin positive imperatives in the *tú* and *vosotros* forms: CL *clamā* > Sp. *llama*, CL *clamāte* > Sp. *llamad*, as well as the Vulgar Latin use of *non* + *subjunctive* for the negative (*no llames, no llaméis*).

b. The positive imperatives require a few special notes concerning their phonological features.

First, among those -*ir* verbs which have a vowel alternation (*servir–sirvo, mentir–miento, dormir–duermo*), analogy was as much at work in the *tú* imperatives as it was in the present indicative (§176a-d). The *tú* imperatives of these verbs, instead of developing to their normal phonetic result, were based on the strong forms of the present indicative. Thus, the *tú* commands *sirve, miente* and *duerme* are analogical with *sirvo, miento* and *duermo*. If normal phonetic evolution had taken place, CL *sĕrvī, mĕntī* and *dŏrmī* would have developed to a hypothetical Sp. *serve, sente* and *dorme* since final long *i* raises a preceding open vowel one step up the vowel triangle. (§110), and thus would impede diphthongization.

c. In Classical Latin, there were a few *tū* imperatives which had no ending at all, for example *fac* (from *facĕre*), *dīc* (from *dīcĕre*), *dūc* 'lead!' (from *dūcĕre*) and *es* (from *esse*). Of these, only *dīc* has survived into Spanish: *di*. It is possible that *di* had an analogical influence on other common commands, causing them to lose their final *e* by analogy, contrary to §95b.

> VL dịc > Sp. di
> VL face > Sp. haz
> VL pone > Sp. pon
> VL salị > Sp. sal
> VL tenị (CL *tĕnē*) > Sp. ten
> VL vẹnị > Sp. ven

Teni was apparently analogical with *veni*; the CL *tĕnē*, with no final *i* to prevent diphthongization, would have developed to *tien(e)*. CL *fac* would have developed to Sp. *fa* (§147a).

d. Finally, mention must be made of *ve (ir)* and *sé (ser)*. VL *vade* replaced the extremely short Classical imperative *ī*, and lost its *d* and gave this development: *vade* > *vai* > *vei* > *ve*. The plural command of *īre (īte)* was continued into Spanish: *id*. The imperative forms of VL *esse (es* and *este)* were lost and replaced in Vulgar Latin by the imperatives of *sedere* (VL *sede* and *sedete*), which, through normal phonetic evolution, gave Sp. *sé* and *sed*.

The Inchoative Flexion

§187a. The inchoative flexion (§49ab) which gained new members in Vulgar Latin while losing its inceptive notion, continued to gain new members on the way to Spanish. In the inchoative conjugation, the first person singular ending, *-sco*, should have developed to *-sco* in Spanish as well, but due to an analogy, it developed to *-zco*.

VL paresco > OSp. paresco > Sp. parezco
VL paresces > Sp. pareces
VL parescet > Sp. parece
VL parescemus > Sp. parecemos
VL parescetis > Sp. parecéis
VL parescent > Sp. parecen

This is one instance where the first person singular yielded to analogical pressure applied by the rest of the conjugation. Since the consonant before the ending in inchoative verbs developed to [θ] everywhere but in the first person singular, where it was [s], this latter form gave in, and changed its etymological *-sco* for an analogical *-zco*.

b. There were a number of verbs represented both by *-ir* and inchoative infinitives in Old Spanish, and in most every case the inchoative is the only form to survive:

(CL dormīre)   OSp. adormir—adormesçer
(CL fallĕre)   OSp. fallir—fallesçer
(CL florēre)   OSp. florir—floresçer
(CL offerre)   OSp. ofrir—ofresçer
(CL patī)   OSp. padir—padesçer
(CL perīre)   OSp. perir—peresçer
(CL stabilīre)   OSp. establir—establesçer

Of the double infinitives, only *aburrir* and *aborrecer* (from CL *abhorrēre*) survive in both forms in Spanish since the two became differentiated semantically.

c. The inchoative flexion became quite aggressive in Old Spanish, imposing itself onto verbs which were never inchoative, but merely happened to have an infinitive ending in *-cer* or *-cir*. VL *jacer, jaco* (CL *jaceō*) developed fairly regularly in Old Spanish to *yaçer, yago*, but soon the inchoative flexion infiltrated into this verb, and the modern outcome is *yacer, yazgo*. Other examples include:

Vulgar Latin	Spanish
cognoscere, cognosco	conocer, conozco
complacere, complaco	complacer, complazco
conducire, conduco	conducir, conduzco
reducire, reduco	reducir, reduzco
traducire, traduco	traducir, traduzco

Cognoscere, although it looks as if it might have originally been an inchoative verb, was not (the *o* of *-oscere* is the clue—no inchoative had an *-oscere* infinitive).

d. Many new verbs which were built on nouns or adjectives went to the inchoative flexion, much of the time with the addition of the prefix *en- (em-)*.

(bello)	embellecer
(blanco)	emblanquecer
(claro)	clarecer
(favor)	favorecer
(mane = *mañana*)	amanecer
(negro)	negrecer
(oscuro)	oscurecer
(pobre)	empobrecer
(rico)	enriquecer
(tarde)	tardecer
(verde)	verdecer
(viejo)	envecejer

Outcome of the Future Passive and Present Active Participles

§188. The accusative case of Classical Latin future passive participles (one of its uses is shown in §75a), also called the GERUND, survived in Spanish as the present participle or gerund:

> CL clamandum > Sp. llamando
> CL bibĕndum > Sp. bebiendo
> CL movĕndum > Sp. moviendo
> CL audiĕndum > Sp. oyendo

Of the four conjugations, only the *-ire* group had a Vulgar Latin yod; this yod remained and was able to raise a pretonic *e* to *i* or *o* to *u*:

VL dormiendu > Sp. durmiendo
VL metiendu > Sp. midiendo
VL moriendu > Sp. muriendo
VL serviendu > Sp. sirviendo
VL veniendu > Sp. viniendo
VL vestiendu > Sp. visitieno

The gerunds from the Classical Latin second and third conjugations were later to develop a yod due to the diphthongization of the open *e*: *moviendo*, *bebiendo*, but this yod developed too late to raise the preceding vowel; the *-ire* yod had a head start of a number of centuries to effect its raising influence.

The Classical Latin verb *posse* (VL *potére*) had no future passive participle, so the gerund of Sp. *poder* had to be specially constructed; it was built on the preterite root: *pudiendo*. In Old Spanish gerunds were commonly built on the preterite stem: *toviendo*, *dixiendo*, *oviendo*, *supiendo*. All of these except *pudiendo* reverted to their normal developments in modern Spanish (*teniendo*, *diciendo*, *habiendo*, *sabiendo*); *pudiendo* could not change, however, since it had no etymological form to fall back on.

CL *esse* 'to be' had no future passive participle either. Sp. *siendo* derives from *sedendu* of *sedere*.

The future passive participle of CL *íre* was *eundum*, which was 'regularized' to *iendu* in Vulgar Latin to give *yendo* in Spanish.

Syntactically, the Classical Latin notion of the gerund was carried into Spanish, as seen in this example: *Yendo a Madrid, hice mucho*. But also, the gerund gave rise to the progressive tenses in Spanish: *Estoy leyendo, siguen durmiendo, iban trabajando*.

§189. The Classical Latin present active participle has survived as a noun or adjective, having lost its verb quality:

CL cantāntem > Sp. cantante
CL ponēntem > Sp. poniente
CL tenēntem > Sp. teniente
CL dormiēntem > Sp. durmiente

The diphthong *ie* of Sp. *teniente* and *poniente* has no etymological basis (owing to the long *e* in Classical Latin) but is rather analogical with the *-ire* conjugation or with the gerunds.

The Latin yod of the *-ire* group was again able to raise the preceding *e* or *o* in all cases: *sirviente* (< *sěrviēntem*), *durmiente*.

The Imperfect Indicative

§190a. The Classical Latin -*āba*- endings came into Spanish intact, but the CL *(i)ēba*- endings simplified to -*ea* in Vulgar Latin (§57b); phonetic result in Spanish is -*ía*-.

In the examples below, it should be noticed that the stress, which varied in Latin, regularized over the same vowel in Spanish in every conjugation:

VL clamába > Sp. llamaba
VL clamábas > Sp. llamabas
VL clamábat > Sp. llamaba
VL clamabámus > Sp. llamábamos
VL clamabátis > Sp. llamabais
VL clamábant > Sp. llamaban

VL debéa (CL *debēbam*) > Sp. debía
VL debéas > Sp. debías
VL debéat > Sp. debía
VL debeámus > Sp. debíamos
VL debeátis > Sp. debías
VL debéant > Sp. debían

VL bibéa (CL *bibēbam*) > Sp. bebía
VL bibéas > Sp. bebías
VL bibéat > Sp. bebía
VL bibeámus > Sp. bebíamos
VL bibeátis > Sp. bebíais
VL bibéant > Sp. bebían

VL dorméa (CL *dormiēbam*) > Sp. dormía
VL dorméas > Sp. dormías
VL dorméat > Sp. dormía
VL dormeámus > Sp. dormíamos
VL dormeátis > Sp. dormíais
VL dorméant > Sp. dormían

The *vosotros* form -*abais* did not simplify from OSp. -*ábades* until the seventeenth century. (In the present indicative, OSp. -*ades* simplified to -*ais* in the fifteenth century, §171.)

b. In the thirteenth century, sometimes the imperfect of the -*er* and -*ir* verbs changed their endings and stress: -*ía* first became -*ie* as the *a* assimilated to the *i*, then the stress moved to the *e* (as in

CL *mulíerem* > VL *muliére*). The first person singular withstood this change, however:

tenía	teniémos
teniés	teniédes
tenié	tenién

This stress pattern is borne out by two facts. First, some forms show an inflected pretonic vowel due to the newly formed yod: OSp. *sirvié* for *servía*. Second, the imperfect ending *-ie* rimed with *é*, which proves it had to be pronounced *-ié* and not *-íe*.

c. The irregular imperfects in Spanish inherit their irregular features from Classical Latin.

The development of the imperfect of CL *esse* into Spanish shows no diphthongization of the CL *ĕ* because of the unstressed nature of the verb *ser*:

CL éram > Sp. era	CL eŕrámus > Sp. éramos
CL éras > Sp. eras	CL erátis > Sp. erais
CL érat > Sp. era	CL ˤrant > Sp. eran

The irregular imperfect of CL *íre* was continued in Spanish, and developed normally:

CL íbam > Sp. iba	CL ibámus > Sp. íbamos
CL íbas > Sp. ibas	CL ibátis > Sp. ibais
CL íbat > Sp. iba	CL íbant > Sp. iban

The Spanish irregular imperfect *veía* reflects the *regular* outcome of the imperfect of *veer* in Old Spanish. There was no phonetic reason for *veía* to lose any vowel (as there was in such forms as *veer, vee, veemos,* where two like vowels merged) so it was carried over into modern Spanish intact.

The Outcome of the Perfect

§191a. The weak perfects of Vulgar Latin from the *-are* conjugation (§58a) developed normally into Spanish:

VL clamái > Sp. llamé
VL clamásti > Sp. llamaste
VL clamáut > Sp. llamó
VL clamámus > Sp. llamamos
VL clamástis > OSp. llamastes > Sp. llamasteis
VL clamárunt > Sp. llamaron

The Old Spanish second person plural ending -stes is etymological; the change to -steis in modern Spanish is analogical with all other tenses where there is an i in the vosotros ending.

b. Old Spanish retained the double development in the plural from the Vulgar Latin -ire conjugation (§58a), but modern Spanish has kept only *one* form for each person. The first and second person plural forms derive from those Vulgar Latin forms which had left out the Classical -vi-, while the third person plural form is based on the Vulgar Latin form which eliminated only the -v-:

Classical Latin	Vulgar Latin	Old Spanish	Modern Spanish
partí(v)ī	partíi	partí	partí
parti(ví)stī	partísti	partiste	partiste
partív(i)t	partíut	partió	partió
partí(v)imus	partiémus	partiemos	———
partí(vi)mus	partímus	partimos	partimos
partī(v)ístis	partiéstis	partiestes	———
partī(ví)stis	partístis	partistes	partisteis
partī(v)ērunt	partiérunt	partieron	partieron
partī(vē)runt	partírunt	partiron	———

In Old Spanish, those plural forms in the -ir conjugation which had a yod regularly raised the preceding e to i, or the preceding o to u. However, the plural forms which had no yod could not inflect the preceding e or o; thus:

Vulgar Latin	Old Spanish	Vulgar Latin	Old Spanish
petiemus	pidiemos	petimus	pedimos
petiestis	pidiestes	petiste	pedistes
petierunt	pidieron	petirunt	pediron
dormiemus	durmiemos	dormimus	dormimos
dormiestis	duirmiestes	dormistes	dormistes
dormierunt	dumieron	dormirunt	dormiron

Modern Spanish, which has retained the yod only in the third person plural, shows an inflected vowel only in that plural form.

In the singular, where VL -íut yielded -ió, inflection was universal: petíut > pidió, dormíut > durmió.

§192. Of the remaining two Classical Latin conjugations (-*ēre* and -*ĕre*), only the -*ēre* group had weak perfects, and there were only very few of them (§58b). The few that there were either disappeared from the language (*delēre, delēvī* 'destroy', for example, was not continued) or changed conjugation groups (*implēre, implēvī* 'fill', became *henchir, henchí; complēre, complēvī* 'complete', became *cumplir, cumplí*, for example). Spanish has not inherited a single -*ere* weak perfect from Classical Latin, yet there are a great number of weak perfects belonging to the Spanish -*er* conjugation. It is evident, then, that a large percentage of Classical Latin strong perfects were rebuilt based on the weak system, as will now be explained.

The Development of Strong Perfects

§193. When a Classical Latin strong perfect (mostly of the -*ēre* and -*ĕre* conjugations) was rebuilt on a weak pattern, it took the endings of the -*ire* weak perfects owing to the phonetic and formal similarities between the conjugations involved.

In Classical Latin, the strong perfects really only had three 'strong' forms, generally speaking; the first and third person singular and the first person plural. (In §58cd there are good examples of this.) In Spanish, the strong preterites have only *two* strong forms: the first and third person singular. The plural forms, now all weak, took analogical -*ir* weak endings.

The remarks that have been made in this section can be applied to all sections that follow dealing with the perfect.

§194a. Those strong -*u*- perfects (§58b) which changed to fit the weak pattern, show the development that follows. Examples are from CL *timēre*:

Classical Latin	Vulgar Latin	Spanish
tímuī	timíi	temí
timuístī	timísti	temiste
tímuit	timíut	temió
timúimus	timímus	temimos
timístis	timístis	temisteis
timuḗrunt	timiérunt	temieron

The Spanish examples show the -*ire* endings described in the preceding section. If the strong conjugation had been maintained, the forms would have been quite confusing: the third person singular and the first person plural would have duplicated the present indicative forms: *teme, tememos.*

Other strong *-u-* perfects that became weak include: *aperīre (apéruī > abrí), cooperīre (coopéruī > cubrí), debēre (débuī > debí) dolēre (dóluī > dolí), jacēre (jácuī > yací), valēre (váluī > valí). Merēre (méruī)* and *parēre (páruī)* became inchoatives (and therefore weak) in Spanish: *merecer (merecí)* and *parecer (parecí).*

b. The strong *-u-* perfects which remained strong were due to undergo quite a bit of change in order to do so, and their resulting history is somewhat complex.

The logical place to start with the development of the perfect of *habēre* from Classical Latin to Old Spanish:

Classical Latin	Old Spanish
hábuī	ove
habuístī	oviste
hábuit	ovo
habúimus	oviemos
habuístis	oviestes
habuḗrunt	ovieron

In this verb, as with VL *cápuī* (CL *cépī*) and CL *sápuī* below, the wau (*-u-*) has been attracted to the preceding vowel and has mixed with it to yield *o*: CL *hábuī* > VL *aubī* > OSp. *ove*. (*V* is merely a variant graph for the *b* sound.) This process is similar to the one where a yod is attracted to and mixes with a preceding vowel, as in *capio > caipo > queipo > quepo, sapiat > saipat > seipa > sepa* (§109). The other *-u-* perfects with an *a* in the stem were VL *cápuī* > OSp. *cope* and CL *sapuī* > OSp. *sope*.

One notices that the third person *habuit* should have developed to *ove*, but if it had, it would have been exactly like the first person singular form. The weak conjugations provided an analogical *o* to avoid this confusion. The final unstressed *o* is a universal feature in all 'strong' Spanish preterites (except *fue*).

This particular perfect, that of *habēre*, was to have an analogical influence on a few Spanish verbs. CL *ténuī* (from *tenēre* 'to hold') never gave *tene* in Old Spanish; instead, it modeled itself after *ove* and became *tove*. Similarly, the reduplicated perfect *stétī* (from *stāre*), while yielding its normal development, *estide*, in Old Spanish, also developed an analogical preterite based on *ove*: *estove*. The myste-

mysterious andar equally developed an analogical preterite: *andove*.
Old Spanish occasionally showed other analogical *-ove* preterites:
crove from *creer* and *crecer, sove* from *ser.*

OSp. *ove, tove, cope, estove* and *andove* still require a further
development to become the modern *hube, tuve, cupe, estuve* and
anduve, as will be explained now.

c. When the wau of the Classical Latin perfects *pótuī* (from CL
posse) and *pósuī* (from CL *pónĕre* 'to place') mixed with the preceding *o,* the result was *u*:

Classical Latin	Old Spanish	Classical Latin	Old Spanish
pótuī	pude	pósuī	puse
potuístī	pudiste	posuístī	pusiste
pótuit	pudo	pósuit	puso
potúimus	pudimos	posúimus	pusimos
potuístis	pudistes	posuístis	pusistes
potuḗrunt	pudieron	posuḗrunt	puisieron

Pude and *pudo* are seen in the earliest Spanish texts.

The *u* of these two verbs was very powerful, and caused all of
the verbs in the preceding section to exchange their etymological *o*
for an analogical *u*:

Old Spanish			Modern Spanish
ove			hube
tove			tuve
cope	+ puse	=	cupe
sope	pude		supe
estove			estuve
andove			anduve

§195a. Among the sigmatic perfects (§58c), a number were lost
early and were rebuilt on the weak pattern, using the infinitive's
stem, and taking the weak *-ir* endings:

> CL ardḗre, ársī > Sp. arder, ardí
> CL erigĕre, eréxī > Sp. erguir, erguí
> CL torquḗre, tórsī > Sp. torcer, torcí

b. Other sigmatic perfects were common in Old Spanish, but
were finally ousted and new weak perfects were rebuilt, based on
the infinitive:

Classical Latin	Old Spanish	Spanish
cingĕre, cínxī	ceñir, cínxe	ceñir, ceñí
coquĕre, cóxī	cocer, cóxe	cocer, cocí
mittĕre, mísī	meter, míse	meter, metí
ridĕre, rísī	reír, ríse	reír, reí
scrībĕre, scrípsī	escribir, escrísse	escribir, escribí
tingĕre, tínxī	teñir, tínxe	teñir, teñí

c. The few sigmatic perfects that have survived into modern Spanish were CL *díxī* *(dīcĕre)*, compounds of CL *dúxī* *(dūcĕre)*, VL *quési* [for CL *quaesívī*] *(quaerĕre)*, and *tráxī* *(trahĕre)*.

Classical Latin	Spanish	Classical Latin	Spanish
díxī	dije	tradúxī	traduje
dīxístī	dijiste	tradūxístī	tradujiste
díxit	dijo	tradúxit	tradujo
díximus	dijimos	tradúximus	tradujimos
dīxístis	dijisteis	tradūxístis	tradujisteis
dīxḗrunt	dijeron	tradūxḗrunt	tradujeron

The third person plural of these verbs in Old Spanish (*dixieron, traduxieron* [dišyéron, traðušyéron]) show a yod which was eventually swallowed up by the palatal [š]. The yod was equally swallowed up, it should be mentioned, by the palatals which end the stems in the modern Spanish preterites of the *ciñeron* and *bulleron* type.

Other compounds of *dūcĕre* include: *aducir, conducir, deducir, introducir, producir.*

VL *quési* appears to have had a close *e* which was raised by the final close *i* to yield modern Spanish *quise*. The phonetic outcome of *tráxī* should have been *treje* (§143), but the *a* is analogical with that of *traer.*

§196a. Among the third type of strong perfects, which usually showed only a vowel inflection (§58d), all but three were rebuilt based on the infinitive and using the endings of the *-ir* weak conjugation. These examples show some of the rebuilt forms:

Classical Latin	Spanish
legĕre, légī	leer, leí
recipĕre, recépī	recibir, recibí
rumpĕre, rúpī	romper, rompí
vincĕre, vícī	vencer, vencí

Sēdī, the strong perfect of *sedēre*, fell out of use and was replaced by the perfect of *esse* (*fuī*), explained below in §198.

b. The three strong perfects pf this type which remained, *vidē-re*, *facĕre* and *venī*re, are given below:

Classical Latin	Spanish	
vídi	vi	
vīdístī	viste	
vídit	vio	
vídimus	vimos	
vīdístis	visteis	
vīdērunt	vieron	

Classical Latin	Old Spanish	Spanish
fécī	fize	hice
fēcístī	feziste	hiciste
fécit	fezo	hizo
fécimus	fezimos	hicimos
fēcístis	fezistes	hicisteis
fēcērunt	fizieron	hicieron
vénī	vine	vine
vēnístī	veniste	viniste
vénit	veno	vino
vénimus	venimos	vinimos
vēnístis	venistes	vinisteis
vēnērunt	vinieron	vinieron

Concerning the preterites of *facĕre* and *venīre*, Old Spanish shows the expected phonetic outcome, with only the first person singular (§110) and the third person plural (§§193, 105) having the right to an inflected vowel. However, as usual, in modern Spanish, the strong first person singular form caused the whole conjugation to take the inflected vowel by analogy.

§197a. All but two of the reduplicated perfects (§58e) were rebuilt on the weak pattern, based on the infinitive. Here are examples of rebuilt reduplicated perfects:

Classical Latin	Spanish
cadĕre, cécidī	caer, caí
credĕre, crédidī	creer, creí
currĕre, curúrrī	correr, corrí
mordĕre, momórdī	morder, mordí
tendĕre, teténdī	tender, tendí
vendĕre, véndidī	vender, vendí

b. The two reduplicated perfects that stayed in the language are *dedī* (from *dare*) and *stetī* (From *stare*). The development of the perfect of *dare* is given below:

CL dédī > Sp. di
CL dĕdístī > Sp. diste
CL dédit > Sp. dio
CL dédimus > Sp. dimos
CL dĕdístis > Sp. disteis
CL déderunt > Sp. dieron

The Spanish conjugation was helped to be 'regular' by analogy with -*ir* endings. (Normal development would have resulted in the diphthongization of the short *e* in the strong forms.)

Stetī can be said to have been continued vicariously, since its normal outcome, OSp. *estide*, was first modified to OSp. *estove*, on the analogy of *ove*, then to Sp. *estuve* on the anology of *pude* (§194bc).

§198. *Fui*, the preterite of both *ser* and *ir* in Spanish, requires some explanation. The perfect of CL *ire* (*iī, īstī, iit, imus, īstis, iērunt*) was destined to be shortlived, owing to its phonological makeup, but why it was replaced by the perfect of *esse* is the question which has to be answered.

The solution goes back to Latin, where, in popular usage, the perfect of *esse* could be used with *in* + *accusative* to mean 'went':

Pretores in provinciam . . . fuerunt.
'The officers went into the province.'

in Mediam fui saepius . . .
'I went more often to Media . . . '

In popular Latin, the accusative case (instead of the ablative) used with a place indicated 'movement toward', so 'the officers were (moving) toward the province' means 'the officers went into the province'. Modern French offers an equivalent of this in its (frowned upon but common) *j'ai été au théâtre* for the more stand-ard *je suis allé(e) au théâtre* 'I went to the theatre'.

Here is the standard development of the conjugation:

CL fúī > Sp. fui
CL fuístī > Sp. fuiste
CL fúit > Sp. fue
CL fuímus > Sp. fuimos
CL fuístis > Sp. fuisteis
CL fuérunt > Sp. fueron

The forms *fui, fuimos* and *fuisteis* have taken analogical *-ir* endings; the modern result through normal development would have been *fue, fuemos, fuiste(i)s* (these forms are actually listed as standard in Nebrija's Spanish grammar of 1492).

The Development of the Imperfect Subjunctive

§199a. Already in Vulgar Latin, the perfect and imperfect sub-junctive, due to a phonetic clash, were beginning to fall and were replaced by the Latin pluperfect subjunctive (§65).

The loss of *-v(i)-* in the perfect (§58a) was universal in Vulgar Latin in the *-are* and *-ire* conjugations. Since the pluperfect subjunc-tive derives from the perfect stem, it, too, lost its *-v(i)-* in the *-are* and *-ire* conjugations:

Vulgar Latin	Spanish
clamá(vi)sse	llamase
clamá(vi)sses	llamases
clamá(vi)sset	llamase
cmama(vi)ssémus	llamásemos
clama(vi)ssétis	llamaseis
clamá(vi)ssent	llamasen
deb(u)ísse	debiese
deb(u)ísses	debieses
deb(u)ísset	debiese
deb(u)issémus	debiésemos
deb(u)issétis	debieseis
deb(u)íssent	debiesen

bibísse	bebiese
bibísses	bebieses
bibísset	bebiese
bibissémus	bebiésemos
bibissétis	bebieseis
bibíssent	bebiesen
dormi(v)ísse	durmiese
dormi(v)ísses	durmieses
dormi(v)ísset	durmiese
dormi(v)issémus	durmiésemos
dormi(v)issétis	durmieseis
dormi(v)íssent	durmiesen

In all cases, the first and second person plural moved their stress back one syllable in Spanish so that the stress would be on the same vowel throughout the conjugation.

In the fourth conjugation, the yod created in the ending inflected the preceding *e* or *o* in the normal way: VL *metiesse* > Sp. *midiese*, VL *moriesse* > Sp. *muriese*.

Again, the *-ire* endings imposed themselves on the *-ere* conjugations. (If the *-ere* forms had developed normally, their conjugations would be based on *debese* and *bebese*.) The Spanish *-er* forms thus have a yod in their endings; however, since the endings were *borrowed*, and did not develop historically from Vulgar Latin times, the *-er* conjugation shows no inflected vowel in the stem.

b. The Classical Latin pluperfect indicative (CL *scrípseram* 'I had written') also built on the perfect stem, retained its pluperfect meaning in Old Spanish (*llamara* 'I had called', *bebiera* 'I had drunk'). When the analytic construction (*había llamado, habías bebido*) began seriously to encroach on the territory of the synthetic pluperfect, the latter began to be used as a *subjunctive*. With the passage of time, it became more important and gained ground to the point where today it is the most common imperfect subjunctive form in Spanish:

VL clama(ve)ra > Sp. llamara
VL deb(u)era > Sp. debiera
VL bibera > Sp. bebiera
VL dormi(v)era > Sp. durmiera

§200. Some mention must be made of the all but extinct future subjunctive in Spanish whose uses (except in legal phrases and in a

few fixed locutions such as *sea lo que fuere*) have been replaced by
the present subjunctive (OSp. *quando viniere* = Sp. *cuando venga*).
The future subjunctive derived from the Classical future perfect
indicative, which was composed of the perfect stem plus the forms
of the future of *esse* as the endings:

VL clama(ve)ro > Sp. llamare
VL clama(ve)ris > Sp. llamares

VL deb(u)ero > Sp. debiere
VL deb(u)eris > Sp. debieres

VL bibero > Sp. bebiere
VL biberis > Sp. bebieres

VL dormi(v)ero > Sp. durmiere
VL dormi(v)eris > Sp. durmieres

The first person singular ending in Spanish is, of course, analogical
with the rest of the conjugation. It should be mentioined that the
etymological outcome, *amaro* (for *amare*) is seen in Berceo, in the
Poema del Cid, and other places.

The Future and Conditional Tenses

§201a. The Vulgar Latin future (§54b), composed of the infinitive followed by the present indicative of *habere*, having replaced
the Classical Latin future, was continued into Spanish:

Vulgar Latin	*Spanish*
clamare + aio	llamaré
debere + aio	deberé
bibere + aio	beberé
dirmire + aio	dormiré

In Old Spanish, it should be mentioned, there were two variants
for the second person plural of *haber: habedes* and *hedes*. It was
the latter form that was used in the formation of the future in
Old Spanish, and has been carried into modern Spanish as *-éis*.

The two part future tense was recognized in Old Spanish,
and the two parts could be therefore separated, as in modern
Portuguese, with a pronoun connected to the infinitive:

darlo e
traervoslo he
darmelo hedes

Separating the future formation with pronouns was not rigidly
observed in any given Old Spanish text. For example, in the *Poema
del Cid*, one sees future forms separated by pronouns as well as
non-separated forms such as this one: *dexaré vos las posadas.*
  b. *Hacer* and *decir* build their future tenses on the old variant
infinitives *far*(modern *har*) and *dïr: haré, diré.*(§169b)
  c. As the two parts of the future formation fused into one
word, the new creation began to act phonetically as one word and
the unstressed *e* or *i* could fall (§102). In Old Spanish, this phenomenon was more common than today, as shown in these examples:

(arder) ardré	(poder) podré
(beber) bevrás	(querer) querrás
(caber) cabrá	(recibir) recibrá
(haber) habremos	(saber) sabremos
(perder) perdrán	(vivir) vivrán

Sometimes, when a vowel fell, two clashing sounds were put
together, and an additional consonant was intercalated in order to
make the cluster pronounceable: *m'r > mbr* (§149b), *n'r > ndr, l'r >
ldr:*

(comer) combré	(tener) tendré
(poner) pondrás	(valer) valdrás
(salir) saldré	(venir) vendrá
(temer) tembremos	

Old Spanish showed an alternate solution to the above; sometimes the two clashing consonants would merely change place,
thus making an easily pronounceable cluster:

(poner) porné
(tener) terné
(venir) verná

In modern Spanish, it is mostly the commonest verbs which
maintain the syncopated form:

(caber) cabré	(saber) saldrás
(haber) habrás	(salir) saldrás
(poder) podrá	(tener) tendrá
(poner) pondremos	(valer) valdremos
(querer) querrán	(venir) vendrán

§202. The development of the conditional tense paralleled that of the future. The endings of the conditional tense derive from the imperfect *endings* of *haber: llamar-ía, deber-ía, beber-ía, dormir-ía, sabr-ía.*

Past Participles

§203a. Of the weak perfect passive participles (§59a), only those of the first and fourth conjugations regularly survived:

Vulgar Latin -are	*Vulgar Latin* -ire
clamátu > llamado	audítu > oído
lavátu > lavado	dormítu > dormido
lucrátu > logrado	ítu > ido
mesurátu > mesurado	partítu > partido
nom(i)nátu ·> nombrado	servítu > servido
plicátu > llegado	vestítu > vestido

b. The weak perfect participles of the Classical Latin *-ēre* conjugation had *-ētum* endings: *completum* 'completed', *delētum* 'destroyed', *implētum* 'filled'. However, no weak *-ēre* perfect passive participles were continued into Spanish; these verbs were either lost (*delētum,* for example), or changed to the *-ire* conjugation group: CL *complētum* = Sp. *cumplido,* CL *implētus* = Sp. *henchido.* This phenomenon parallels the loss of the Classical Latin weak *-ēre* perfects. (§192)

c. The weak past participles of the Classical Latin *-ĕre* conjugation ended in *-ūtus,* and although only a few were continued into Old Spanish (for example, *tribuĕre, tribūtum* > OSp. *(a)trevudo; battuĕre, battūtum* > OSp. *batudo*), the *-udo* ending became very contageous and was spread analogically to a number of verbs. One reads *metudo, vençudo,* in the *Poema del Cid,* and *abatudo, perçebudo, metudo, corrompudo, sabudo, temudo* in the *Libro de Alexandre;* none of these showed *-ūtum* endings in Classical Latin. After the thirteenth century, *-udo* began to be lost (probably because a stressed *u* was otherwise unknown in a Spanish verb ending), and all of these verbs were rebuilt using the *-ido* ending.

A few of the CL *-ūtum* passive participles were retained, but as adjectives: CL *acuĕre, acūtum* > Sp. *agudo;* CL *mĭnuĕre, minūtum* > Sp. *menudo.*

§204. In Vulgar Latin, already a number of Classical Latin strong past participles were made weak, as shown in §60. How-

ever, a certain number of Classical Latin strong participles were
carried into Spanish.

> VL apértu > Sp. abierto
> VL copértu > Sp. cubierto
> VL díctu > Sp. dicho
> VL fáctu > Sp. hecho
> VL fríctu > Sp. frito
> VL mórtu (CL *mortuum*) > Sp. muerto
> VL pósitu > Sp. puesto
> VL rúptu > Sp. roto
> VL scríptu > Sp. escrito
> VL vístu (CL *visum*) > Sp. visto

Some strong participles which carried into Old Spanish were
later made weak, rebuilt on the infinitive:

> CL míssum > OSp. meso / Sp. metido
> CL nátum > OSp. nado / Sp. nacido
> VL quéstu > OSp. quisto / Sp. querido

A few Old Spanish strong participles were maintained in modern Spanish exclusively as adjectives and nouns, while new formations were created for the participle use in modern Spanish:

> VL coctu > OSp. cocho / Sp. cocido
> VL ductu > OSp. ducho / Sp. -ducido
> VL tractu > OSp. trecho / Sp. traído

One sees *cocho* in *biscocho* (lit. 'cooked twice'). The modern *-ducido*
is seen only in compounds (*traducido, introducido,* etc.).

Adverbs

§205a. The Vulgar Latin way of deriving adverbs from adjectives with *-mente* (§68) was continued into Spanish:

> abierta + mente
> lenta + mente
> tranquila + mente

b. A number of Classical Latin adverbs not deriving from adjectives were also continued into Spanish:

CL adhūc > Sp. aún	CL quando > Sp. cuando
CL ante > Sp. antes	CL quōmodo > Sp. como
CL cĭrca > Sp. cerca	CL tantum > Sp. tanto
CL jam > Sp. ya	CL magis > Sp. más

The -n of *aún* is analogical with the -n of *en, con, según, sin*. The -s of *antes* is analogical with the -s of *después, detrás, más, menos*. Other examples of the 'adverbial s' include:

qui sa(be) > quizá (+ s) > quizás
in tunc ce > entonce (+ s) > entonces

c. A number of Classical adverbs were quite short, so prepositions, nouns, or even other adverbs were added to them in Vulgar Latin to give more emphasis or phonetic substance to them:

VL ad fora > Sp. afuera
VL ad hic > Sp. ahí
VL ad illac > Sp. allá
VL ad pressa > Sp. aprisa
VL ad satis > Sp. asáz
VL de ex pŏst > Sp. después
VL de in ante > Sp. delante
VL de trans > Sp. detrás
VL in tunc ce > OSp. entonçe
VL ex tunc ce > OSp. estonçe

Prepositions and Conjunctions

§206a. Most Classical Latin prepositions were continued into Spanish:

CL ad > Sp. a	CL pŏst > Sp. pues
CL ante > Sp. ante	CL pro > Sp. por
CL cĭrca > Sp. cerca	CL secūndum > Sp. según
CL cŭm > Sp. con	CL sĭne > Sp. sin
CL de > Sp. de	CL sŭper > Sp. sobre
CL ĭn > Sp. en	CL trans > Sp. tras
CL ĭnter > Sp. entre	

The development of CL *sĭne* (with short *i*) into Sp. *sin* is unexplained; the normal development in Spanish would have been *sen* (compare Ptg. *sem*). *Sin* could be analogical with a number of short words which have an *i*: *mi, ti, si*.

b. A few Romance prepositions are composed of two or more Classical prepositions.

> de + ex + post > después
> pro + ad > OSp. pora > Sp. para

c. Some Classical prepositions were lost, either because a pair of synonymous prepositions was reduced to only one member for reasons of economy, or, as in the last example below, because a Latin preposition was replaced by one from another source:

> ab, de > Sp. de
> ex, de > Sp. de
> apud, cum > Sp. con
> ob, pro > Sp. por
> versus, facies (VL facia) > Sp. hacia
> tenus, Arab. fatta > Sp. hasta

§207a. A few important Classical conjunctions remained:

> CL ĕt > Sp. y, e
> CL nec > Sp. ni
> CL sī > Sp. si

The development of *et* to OSp. *e* is regular; there was no diphthongization due to the unstressed nature of this conjunction. The modern *y*, however, does present a problem. The following is usually given as the evolution of *y*: the OSp. *e* commonly was found before vowels and would naturally tend to become a yod under this circumstance:

> OSp. e amigos [y amíγos] > Sp. y amigos
> OSp. e obispos [yoβíspos] > Sp. y obispos
> OSp. e uno [yúno] > Sp. y uno

This common case of *e* before vowels (except *i*) is said to have caused *y* to generalize. Before an *i*, however, there was no phonetic reason for the *e* to change its pronunciation, and it is for this reason that modern Spanish maintains *e* before words beginning with [i]: *e hijos, e infantes.*

The development of *nec* to *ni* is obscure, although it could be that it is analogical with *sí*.

b. *Mientras* requires some explanation. *Dum* 'while' and *interim* 'meanwhile' were seen together in popular Latin: *dum ínterim.* With a change in stressed vowels, from an open *i* to an open *e*, the pair developed to *domientre* in Old Spanish. Since many other Old Spanish words began with the more common *de-* (*debaxo, deantes, detrás, después*), *domientre* became *demientre*. Because there were pairs of words, both with and without *de-* (*demás, más; dende, ende; defuera, fuera*), the form *mientre* was created by analogy. Owing to the related words ending in *-a* (*contra, fuera, nunca*), *mientre* became *mientra*. At this point, the 'adverbial *s*' was added, and the modern *mientras* was created.

c. Most Classical Latin conjunctions were lost, however, and were replaced by synonomous conjunctions or others of Romance origin:

CL etsi = Sp. aunque   CL quia = Sp. porque
CL ut = Sp. que   CL ígitur = Sp. por eso
CL sed = Sp. pero   CL cum = Sp. cuando

Having reached the end of this volume, the reader now has, in the estimation of the author, the requisite minimal knowledge of Classical and Vulgar Latin, and of historical phonology and morphology, to allow him or her to begin a profitable study of the more advanced books on this subject.

❧ Select Bibliography ❧

These are some books that the reader might find useful if he or she wants to pursue historical grammar and the history of the Spanish Language. Also included are some standard books dealing with general Romance.

(a) CLASSICAL LATIN

Allen, Joseph Henry and Greenough, James B. *New Latin Grammar.* Boston: Ginn & Co., 1931.

Ernout, A. and Thomas, François. *Syntaxe Latine,* 2e éd., 2e tirage. Paris: Klincksieck, 1959.

Palmer, L. R. *The Latin Language.* London. Faber and Faber, 1954.

Wheelock, Frederick. *Latin: An Introductory Course Based on Ancient Authors,* 3rd ed., New York: Barnes and Noble, 1963.

(b) CLASSICAL LATIN DICTIONARIES

Gaffiot, Félix. *Dictionnaire illustré latin-français.* Paris: Hachette, 1934.

Lewis, Charlton T. and Short, Charles. *A Latin Dictionary.* Oxford: The Clarendon Press, 1966.

(c) VULGAR LATIN

Díaz y Díaz, Manuel. *Antología del latín vulgar,* 2a ed. Madrid: Gredos, 1962.

Grandgent, Charles H. *Introduction to Vulgar Latin.* (rpt.) New York: Hafner, 1962. (Spanish edition, translated by Moll, F. de B., Madrid: 1928.)

Haadsma, R. A. and Nuchelmans, J. *Précis de latin vulgaire.* Gronigen: J. B. Wolters, 1966.

Maurer, Theodoro H., Jr. *O problema do latim vulgar.* Rio de Janeiro: Livraria Acadêmica, 1962.

Rohlfs, Gerhard. *Sermo Vulgaris Latinus,* 2d. ed., Tübingen: Max Niemeyer Verlag, 1956.

Silva Neto, Serafim da. *Fontes do latim vulgar,* 3a ed. Rio de Janeiro: Livraria Acadêmica, 1956.

——————. *História do latim vulgar.* Rio de Janeiro: Livraria Acadêmica, 1957.

Väänänen, Veikko. *Introduction au latin vulgaire.* Paris: Klincksieck, 1963. (Spanish translation of the expanded second French edition published by Gredos.)

157

(d) HISTORICAL GRAMMARS AND HISTORIES OF THE ROMANCE LANGUAGES

Bourciez, Édouard. *Élements de linguistique romane*, 4e éd. Paris: Klincksieck, 1956.

Elcock, W. D. *The Romance Languages*. London, Faber and Faber, 1960.

Lausberg, Heinrich. *Lingüística románica*, Madrid: Gredos, 2 vols., 1965-66.

Meyer Lübke, Wilhelm. *Grammaire des langues romanes*. Paris: E. Welter, 4 vols., 1890-96.

——————. *Introducción al estudio de la lingüística romance*. Madrid: RFE, 1917.

(e) HISTORICAL GRAMMARS AND HISTORIES OF SPANISH

Bolaño e Isla, Amancio. *Manual de historia de la lengua española*. Mexico: Editorial Porrúa, 1959.

Entwistle, William J. *The Spanish Language (together with Portuguese, Catalan and Basque)*, London: Faber and Faber, 1962.

García de Diego, Vicente. *Gramática histórica española*, 3a ed. Madrid: Gredos, 1970.

Hanssen, Federico. *Gramática histórica de la lengua castellana*. Buenos Aires: El Ateneo, 1945.

Lapesa, Rafael. *Historia de la lengua espaóola*, 7a ed. Madrid: Escelicer, 1968.

Menéndez Pidal, Ramón. *Cantar de mío Cid*, 3a ed., 3 vols. Madrid: Espasa-Calpe, 1954-56.

——————. *Manual de gramática histórica española*, 11a ed. Madrid: Espasa-Calpe, 1962.

——————. *Orígenes del español*, 5a ed. Madrid: Espasa-Calpe, 1964.

Otero, Carlos-Peregrín. *Evolución y revolución en romance*, 2 vols. Barcelona: Seix-Barral, 1971 and 1976.

Spaulding, Robert K. *How Spanish Grew*. Berkeley, University of California Press, 1943.

(f) ETYMOLOGICAL DICTIONARIES OF SPANISH

Corominas, Joan. *Breve diccionario etimológico de la lengua castellana*. Madrid: Gredos, 1961.

——————. *Diccionario crítico erumológico de la lengua castellana*, 4 vols. Madrid, 1954-57.

García de Diego, Vicente. *Diccionario etimológico español e hispánico*. Madrid: SAETA, 1955.

ꙮ Word Index ꙮ

All Spanish examples seen in the text are listed below with the exception of verb forms and nouns listed in conjugation and declension models, unless there is something otherwise noteworthy about these examples.

Numbers following the listings refer to *sections*, and not pages. An italicized *n* following a section number refers to the footnote corresponding to that section

NOTE: Spanish alphabetization has been used throughout.

blando 120
bledo 120
boca 4, 114, 132
boda(s) 85, 152b, 155c
bondad 123
brazo 120
bueno 83a, 114, 160a
buey 95d, 149c
buitre 114, 146
buono [OSp.] 83a

C

cabalgar 99b
caballo 90
caber 51a
cabeza(s) 33b, 124a, 152b, 155a
cabezo 115a
cabildo 151b
cabo 82
cabra 82, 124a
cacho 142b
cadena 125a
cadera 17c
caer 129a
caí 58e, 197a
caigo 177a
caldero 109
caldo 102, 129b
caloña 134
callar 133a
calle(s) 152d, 155a
candado 99a, 151b
cantor 90
caña 134
capellán 157b
carácter 156a
caramillo 99a, 149a
cárcel 149a, 152d
carecer 169b
caridad 95a
Carlos 156a
carro 115a
castiello [OSp.] 81b*ii*
castillo 81b*ii*, 115a, 133a, 152c
catorce 166b
cauce 145
caudal 124c
cavar 128a
cebo 128a
cebolla 33c, 85, 89, 115b, 133a, 152b
cedo 97
ceja(s) 80a, 96, 155c
cejar 132d

cejo 141
celo 175b
cena 131
ceñir 169c
cepo 80a, 155b, 132b
cerca 80a, 205b, 206a
cercar 89, 169a
cereza 109, 115b
certidumbre 157b
césped 103
ciego 5, 81a, 126a
cielo 81a
cien(to) 81a, 115a, 166d
cierro 115b
cierto 81a, 115a
ciervo 81a
cigüeña 110, 176a
cilla 133a
cimiento 106
cinco 166a
cincho 142b
cirio 109, 115b
ciudad(es) 88, 95a, 128c, 152d, 155a
claro 121
clave 121
cocido 204
cocho [OSp.] 204
codicia 124c
codo 98, 102, 128c
cojo 143
col 84, 95a, 159a
colgar 169a
coloco 17b, 175
color 95ab, 131
colore 95b
collazo 144c
comenzar 99b
comer 64, 97, 169b
como 156d, 205b
cómo 163
comprar 64, 99a
comprender 51a
compuesto 17b
comulgar 98, 99b, 126a, 149b
comulgo 175
comunico 175
con 147b, 206ab
concebir 51b, 175a
concha 142b
conde 83b, 102, 150b
condestable 156b
conejo 142a
conforta 171b

conmigo 168e
consejo 141
considero 175
construyo 178
contar 150b
contiene 17b
copa 85, 132b
conviene 17b, 77
costumbre 157b
cráter 156a
crecer 135a
cree 95d
creí 173c, 197a
crisis 156a
crudo 129c
cruel 129a, 160b
cruz 95a
cuajo 142a
cuál 163
cuando 13c, 97, 163, 205b, 207c
cuarenta 166c
cuatro 148a, 166a, 167
cuatrocientos 166d
cubierto 204
cuchara 141
cuchiello [OSp.] 81b*ii*
cuchillo 81b*ii*, 146
cuela 171b
cuelga 17b, 77
cuelgo 175
cuello(s) 28b, 133a, 152c, 155b
cuento [verb] 98, 102, 176
cuerno(s) 31, 97, 152c, 155b
cuero 109
cuerpo 148b
cuerpos [OSp. sing.] 148b, 153b
cuesta 171b
cuervo 83a, 115a
cueva 83a
cuévano 127
coraza 136
corlar 151b
corona 91
correa 139
corrí 58e, 197a
cortés 95a
corteza 97
cosa 5, 84
costumbre 149b
costura 99a
coto 125b
coz 145
cuidar 101
culebra 17c
cumbre 145, 149b, 153c

cumplir 176d
cuna 140a, 115a
cupe 194c
curar 92

Ch

chico 115b
chinche 115b

D

dañar 113
daño 134
de 69, 206ac
dé 185d
deber 169b
décimo 167
decir 88, 149d, 169c
dedo 102, 113, 130a
defensa 127
dehesa 127
dejar 143
delante 149a, 205c
delgado 125a, 126a, 160a
despecho 144a
después 69, 205c, 206b
detrás 69, 205c
deuda 113, 128c
dezir [OSp.] 169b
di 147a, 186b, 197b
día 32, 152b
dice 126c, 147a
diciembre 106
dicho 204
dieciséis 166b
diez 95a, 126c, 166a
diezmo 102
dije 143
Dios 156a, 165a
dir(é) 169b
do [OSp.] 179
doblar 124a
doce 98, 166b
dolor 152d
domingo 156b
donde 95c, 163
dormir 105, 169c
dos 166a
doscientos 166d
dozientos [OSp.] 166d
dragón 120, 126a
drapo 132b
ducho [OSp.] 144a, 204
duda 128c
dueña 102

dueño(s) 83b, 113, 134, 152c, 155a
duermo 176e
dureza 92, 136
durmamos 105
durmiendo 105
durmieron 105
duro 86, 113, 160a

E

e 207a
echar 144a
edad 95a
eje 143
ejemplo 143
él 39b, 42, 156a, 158abc
ella(s) 39b, 42, 43, 168c
ello 39b, 147a, 168c
ellos 43, 168c
Elvira 117b
embellecer 187d
embestir 175b
en 206a
encía 117b, 128b
encina 150a
engeño 140a
enjambre 157a, 153
enjuto 144b
ensayo 139, 157a
entendedora 160b
entero 15g, 17c, 160a
entonçe [OSp.] 205c
entonces 205b
entre 148a, 206a
entrega 171b
entregar 151a
entrego 81b*ii*
entriego [OSp.] 81b*ii*
enxiemplo [OSp.] 157a
era [Lat. *area*] 109
era [verb] 190c
eres 180a
es 180a
esa 15b, 162
escribe 122
escribir 169c
escrita 6
escrito 79, 122, 204
escuchar 5a, 146, 157a
escudo 86, 122
escuela 6, 122
ese 15b, 39b, 156a,c 162
eso 162
espalda 151b
España 140a

español 149a
española 153a
esparcir 169c
espárrago 102
espejo 9, 102
especie 154
espécimen 156a
espiga 96, 126a
espíritu 154
esponja 142b*n*
esposo 122
esta 162
está 122, 147a
estable 160b
estaño 140b
estatua 6
este 39b, 156a, 162
esté 185d
Esteban 127
estide [OSp.] 194b
estiércol 149a
estío 128b
esto 147a, 162
estó [OSp.] 179
estonçe [OSp.] 205c
estopa 132b
estove [OSp.] 194b
estrecho 22, 144a, 160a
estrella 122
estuve 194, 197c
extraño 140a, 160a

F

fácil 16
favorecer 187a
fazer [OSp.] 16b
fe 32, 116, 129a, 152d
fechar 169a
feligrés 156b
feliz 160b
feo 5, 80a, 116, 129a, 160a
fiel 95a, 116, 129a, 160b
fiero 131
fiesta(s) 28b, 81a, 116, 155c,
flor 4, 95a, 121
fleco 83b
fotografear 169a
fragua 151d
frango 177b
fregar 119
freír 169c
frente 29a, 83c, 120
fresno 37, 102, 116, 120, 143, 152c
frío 130a

mansedumbre 157b
mar(es) 29b, 95a, 152d, 155b
Marcos 156a
margen 103
mármol 149a
martes 156b
martiello [OSp.] 81b*ii*
martillo 85b*ii*
más 11b, 130a, 205b
mayor 38, 161b
maza 136
me 43, 168b
mecer 135a
medir 175a
mejilla 143
mejor 38, 161b
mejorar 169a
menor 38, 161b
menos 113
mentir 175b
menudo 89, 125a
merecer 49
meollo 129a
mermar 149a
mes 95a
mesa 15a
mesurar 169a
meter 132c
metido 204
mezclar 142b*n*
mi 43, 165b
mí 168b
míi [OSp.] 165b
miedo 81a, 125a
miel 16, 29b, 148a
mientras 207b
miércoles 156b
migo [OSp.] 168e
mil 133b, 166e
milagro 142a, 151a
millón 166e
mío 81b*i*, 165b
miraglo [OSp.] 142a
mismo 160c
modo 129c
moneda 80a, 113, 125a
monte 83b, 113
montés 95a
mordí 197a
moro 84
mosca 85
muchedumbre 157b
mucho 146
mudar 92, 125a, 169a
mudo(s) 86, 97, 113, 160a

muela 83a
muelle 133a
muero 176e
muerte 83a
muerto 204
muestra 159, 171b
muger [OSp.] 168d
mujer 7c, 77, 141
mundo 97
muro 4, 86
muslo 142b*n*
muy 146

N

nacido 204
nada 164
nadie 164
nado [OSp.] 204
ni 147a
nido 129c
niebla 81a, 102, 113
nieta 113
nieve 128
ninguno 164
noble 95c, 98
noche 144a
nodrir 113
nombrar 91, 113, 169a
nombre 149b, 153c
nos 43
nos [OSp.] 168ab
nosotros 41, 168a
novecientos 166d
noveno 167
noventa 166c
novio 137a
nube 128a
nublar 92, 128a
nuera 31
nuestro 165b
nueva 113
nueve 4, 83a, 128a, 166a
nuevo 128a
nuez 95a, 126c
nunca 10, 164

O

o 147a
obedecer 169c
obra 29c
oca 84, 126b
ocasionar 169a
otavo 167
ochavo 67

ochenta 166c
ocho 166a
ochcientos 166d
oí 129a
oigo 177a
oír 129a, 169c
odre 125a
ojo 9, 102, 142a
olvidar 151a
once 166b
orebze [OSp.] 127
oreja(s) 33b, 142a, 152b
os 43, 168b
osar 131
oso 15d
otero 145
otoño 97, 125b, 134
otro 98, 102, 145
ove [OSp.] 58b, 111, 194b
oveja 33c

oyo [OSp.] 178

P

pacer 135a
padre(s) 82, 95c, 113, 125a, 148b
paga 126a, 107, 113
pájaro 132d, 141
palabra 113, 131, 151a
pan 95a
paño 134
para 206b
paraíso 99a
parecer 49, 187a, 169b
pared 7c, 29a, 90, 95a, 152d
parienta 153a
parir 51b, 169c
parte 95c
partir 90, 169c
parto 175a
paso 132d
pastor 95a
pastora 153a
paz 126c
pebre 153c
pecar 132a
pecho 144a, 148b
pechos [OSp. sing.] 148b, 153b
pedir 169c
peine 113, 144c
peligro 151a
pelo 131
pelliza 136
pena 80a
peor 38, 161b

pera(s) 28c, 131, 152b, 155c
perdiz 95a
pereza 15g
pero 207c
pescar 89
pescuezo 136
pesuña 156b
pez 135b
pie 81a, 129a
piedra 81a, 125a
piel 81a, 133b
piélago 102
piensa 171b
pierdo 81a
pierna(s) 152b, 155a
piezgo 102, 129b
pino 31, 131
piña 134, 140a
piñón 95a
plango 177b
plaza 82, 121, 136
plazo 126c
pluma 121
pobre 35c, 84, 124a, 160b
poblar 99a
poco 84, 126b
poder 95a
podre 85, 125a
pollo 85, 133a
pon 186b
pondré 150c
poner 51a, 169b
pongo 177b
popa 132b
por 69, 206ac
por eso 207c
porque 207c
portaje 157b
portazgo 157b
posar 91
poyo 138a
pozo 85, 136
prado 4, 120, 125a
pregón 89, 95a
presto 171c
primer 167
prisión 109
probar 128
propio 149c
provecho 144a
pude 94, 194c
pudiendo 188
pudor 11a
puarta [OSp.] 83a
puebla 102

traído 204
traidor 101
traigo 177a
traje 195c
trapo 120
tras 206a
través 95a, 149c
trébol 127
trece 166b
treinta 11b, 130a, 166c
trecho [OSp.] 204
tres 166a
trescientos 166d
trezientos [OSp.] 166d
tribu 154
trigo 11a
triste 35b
troncho 142b
trucha 144a
tu 165b
tú 86, 156a
túe [OSp.] 165b
tuorto [OSp.] 83a
turbio 108, 129a
tuve 194c

U

uamne [OSp.] 83a
un(o)(s) 86, 159, 166a
uña 142b*n*
uso 131
usted 168a

V

vaamos [OSp.] 185b
vacío 114, 128b
vaca 114, 132a
vado 129c
vajilla(s) 155c
valdré 150c
valgo 177bvalle 133a
vamos 180b
vaya 185b
ve [ir] 186d
veces 4
vecino 126c, 149d
veda 171b
veer [OSp.] 190c
vega 107
veinte 11b, 130a, 166c
vello 133a
ven 186b
vender 51a, 95a, 169b

vendí 197a
vendré 150c
venir 95a
venga [vengar] 102
vengar 126a, 150b
vengo [vengar] 175
vengo [venir] 177a
venir 169c
veo 172
ver 129a, 169b, 172
verdad(es) 125a, 155a
verde 102, 129b, 160b
vergüenza 99a, 109, 138b
vestir 175b
veta 132c
veyo [OSp.] 172
vez 126c
vía 80b
viaje 157b
vid 79, 125a
vida 114, 125a
vidrio 125a
viejo 9, 142b
viernes 151b, 156b
vil 95a
vindico 175
vine 94, 110
vino(s) 28b, 79, 97, 114, 152c, 155b
viña 79
virtud 95a
visto 60, 204
vivir 128a, 169c
vo [OSp.] 179, 180b
vos [OSp.] 168a
vosotros 41, 168a
voy 180b
voz 126c
vuestra merced 168a
vuestro 165b

Y

y 207a
ya 118a, 164, 205b
yace 118a
yacer 118a, 168d
Yagüe 118a
yazgo 187c
yegua 81a
yente [OSp.] 117c*n*
yerma 102
yermo 81a
yerno 117, 151b
yo 156a, 168

❧ Index ❧

Numbers following entries refer to pages.
Page numbers for definitions are in italics